Michael Strauss

Value Creation in Travel Distribution

ISBN 978-0-557-61246-8

© Copyright 2010 Michael Strauss
All rights reserved.
PASS IT-Consulting Dipl.-Inf. G. Rienecker GmbH & Co.KG

Preface

From a technological point of view, the travel industry is not the hunter, but the prey. Innovations are neither fostered nor developed to the extent necessary. Suppliers, distributors and travel management companies, are partially to blame for this, as are technology providers. However, new concepts can help the travel industry reduce costs, master crises and offer better products.

The long term future of the travel industry is secure. Due to progressive globalization, the demand for mobility will also continue to grow in the future. However, the travel industry must live with various setbacks: terrorist attacks, epidemics and the financial crisis. Everything impacts the travel industry and vice versa: If the travel industry is weak, it influences all other industries as well. A strike by airline employees or a volcano eruption leads to serious impacts on every global business.

This book's in-depth analysis reveals the fragility of the travel industry's stability from a perspective of distribution and information technology (IT). In other industries technology sets the pace for innovation, while in the travel industry it seems to be lagging behind. The travel industry has a huge potential to use many more options that would make it more resistant to future fluctuations and also would result in new attractive products and processes. A more sophisticated level of enthusiasm regarding innovation as seen in other industries would strengthen the future ability of its existing distribution players to survive.

The distribution struggle in the travel industry is also not exactly conducive to innovation. We can observe markets cannibalizing themselves and airlines distributing directly by disintermediation of the Global Distribution Systems and possibly even agencies or Travel Management Companies. For instance, Global Distribution Systems provide booking tools for brick and mortar agents, while at the same time they operate Online Travel Agencies in competition. Nowadays Global Distribution Systems are very selective with their certified developers. Some practices are even investigated by the Department of Justice. Consumers and corporations may pay a premium for distribution that new entrants could significantly reduce. American Airlines has already started the migration of their full content to direct channels enabled by XML and third-party technology firms. This means American Airlines has taken the first step towards independence from Global Distribution Systems. Thus, one can conclude that American Airlines punishes traditional distributors, which are driven mainly by political decisions and fruitless negotiations, by reducing their market share.

Meanwhile, most airlines are struggling to return to profitability, while low-cost providers Southwest Airlines and JetBlue continue to set the standard for air travel. Legacy airlines are thus unbundling their full service fare and charge extra for bags, blankets, seat reservations and even overhead bin space. This ancillary revenue is expected to play a major role in future balance sheets of airlines.

The past decade was dominated by travelers booking their trips online. Online sites like Travelocity, Priceline and Orbitz steer millions of consumers toward specific airlines and hotels in a manner that lowers prices and improves satisfaction among consumers. However, the coming years might be influenced by mobile booking. With more than half of the US public using smart phones and high speed cellular networks, the basis for this scenario has already been established. The more important question becomes if travel industry players will enable mobile value added services for their clients or if an experienced online and mobile provider will step up. Usually Internet giants such as Apple, Google and Microsoft do not wait until an industry is ready for a change – as painfully experienced by the music industry.

Based on industry developments as those described above, this book serves as a guide to the fascinating travel sector from a global perspective, offering insights into the economic, political, and social forces that drive and shape tourism through the power of distribution.

The travel industry has been through exceptional upheaval and change. This book provides well-researched access to the complete scope of the travel industry including: Analysis of the industry's status quo as well as major trends; Market research; Statistics and historical tables; Airlines' roles; and distributors' and travel agents' positions in the present and in the future.

Table of Contents

Table of Contents
Table of Figures
1 Introduction to the travel industry 1
   1.1 The structure of the travel industry 1
   1.2 Distribution & inventory management in detail 5
   1.3 Airline incentive model and clearing 9
   1.4 Figures for the travel market 10
   1.5 History 12
2 Current situation 19
   2.1 The travel experience today 19
   2.2 Strengths 23
   2.3 Weaknesses 24
   2.4 The necessary change – innovation and quality 25
   2.5 Challenges 32
   2.6 Opportunities 34
3 Trends 35
   3.1 Cell phones / Mobiles 35
   3.2 Direct distribution 39
   3.3 Virtual meetings / Video conferences 40
   3.4 Going green 42
   3.5 Ancillary fees via merchandising 45
   3.6 Social media and travel 50
   3.7 Door-to-door, Geo data and trip management 55
   3.8 Further trends 56
4 Future scenario 1: evolution 61
   4.1 Suppliers 61
   4.2 Distribution 63
   4.3 Sales 66
   4.4 End users and businesses 73
   4.5 Technology and target architecture 75
5 Future scenario 2: Revolution 81
   5.1 Revolution initiated by an industry expert 81
   5.2 Revolution initiated by a newcomer outside the sector 83
   5.3 Revolution initiated by a newcomer outside the region: 86
6 Future scenario 3: revolution with evolution 89
7 Glossary 93
8 Footnotes 95

Table of Figures

Figure 1: Travel Value Chain..1
Figure 2: Travel distribution landscape..2
Figure 3: Airline incentive model...9
Figure 4: Travel market worldwide...10
Figure 5: US Travel Market per segment..11
Figure 6: Players in the value creation segment..25
Figure 7: Classical representation of players..26
Figure 8: Current representation of players..27
Figure 9: Innovation check of travel compared to other industries..30
Figure 10: Direct distribution supplier savings..39
Figure 11: Carbon dioxide offset requirements..42
Figure 12: Ancillary Revenue (airlines)..46
Figure 13: Door-to-door locations..55
Figure 14: Flexible travel distribution technology architecture..79

1 Introduction to the travel industry

1.1 The structure of the travel industry

Figure 1: Travel Value Chain

The travel market, like any other industry, is based on supply and demand. The supply side is differentiated into providers for air travel, cars, hotels, cruises, rail travel, etc. Demand arises from end customers who act via an agent for the most part in order to obtain an adequate overview of the multitude of offers. Thus the value chain in the travel industry can be divided into five parts:

1. Suppliers: airlines, hotels, car rental companies, etc.
2. Inventory management: administration of the inventory in a CRS[1]
3. Distribution: usually Global Distribution Systems (GDSs), but also aggregators[2], consolidators[3] and organizers
4. Sales: End customers can arrange their travel purchase through the agency/TMC[4], one of the online agencies (OTA[5], OTMC[6]) or even the provider directly on the corresponding website (direct).
5. Market: the traveler[7] or the company.

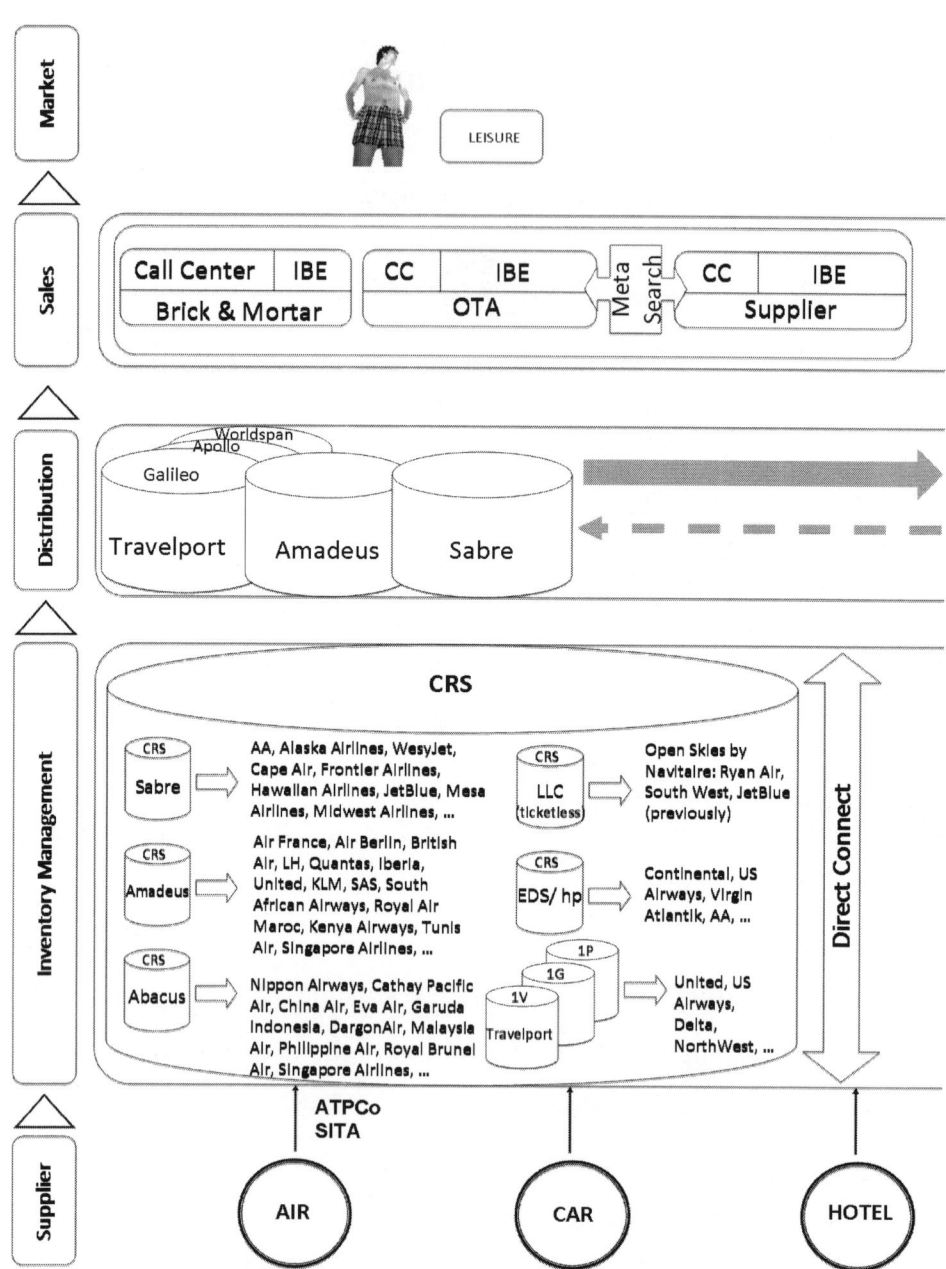

Figure 2: Travel distribution landscape

Value Creation in Travel Distribution   Michael Strauss

BUSINESS

Call Center	OBT
TMC	

CC	Corp. IBE
OTA	

CC	Corp. IBE
Supplier	

Market Place/
Distribution Channel:
- Consolidator
- Aggregator
- Tour Operator

→ CarTrawler, RentaCar,....,
→ Pegasus, HRS, Hotel.com,
  Hotel.de, Booking.com/
  Priceline.com, ...
→ Packages: Flight, Hotel, Car,
  Cruise, Sightseeing, ...

Direct Connect

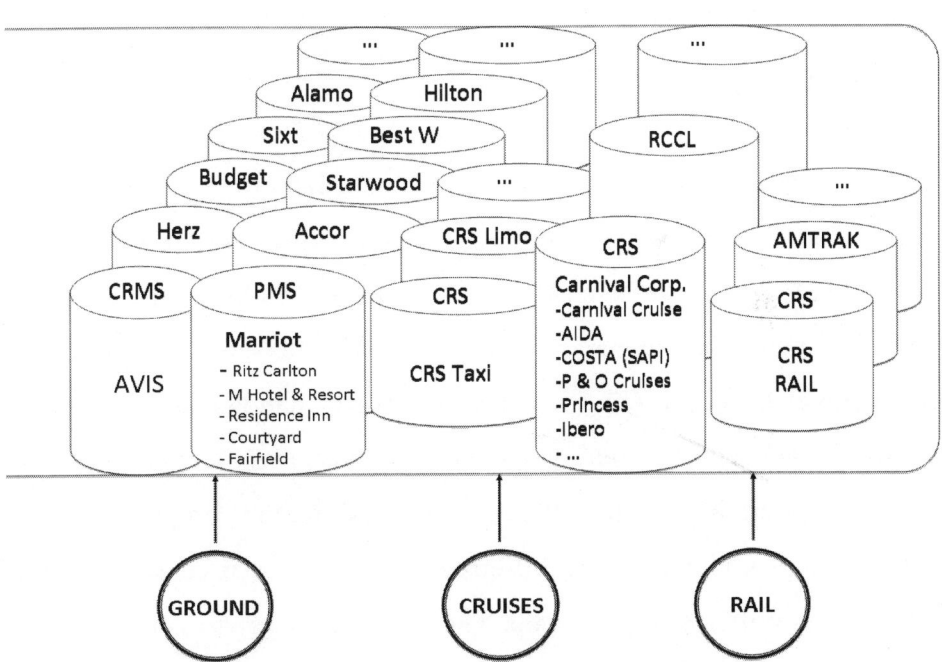

Rates are usually administered by airlines via ATPCo[8] or SITA[9]. Here the fare rules are stored together with the price information of each fare, i.e., the price for a seat in an aircraft in a certain class[10]. ATPCo markets these fares to the GDSs. Published and negotiated fares (net or nego fares) can be managed in ATPCo. However, there are also other providers of net fare databases.

The inventory is managed in central reservation systems (CRSs) and distributed via global distribution systems (GDSs). The established GDSs usually operate the CRSs, so most people consider the terms GDS and CRS to be synonymous. However, in this document inventory management (CRS) and distribution (GDS) are considered as two distinct steps of value creation.

Sales are handled by agencies or direct distribution. A distinction is usually made between leisure and business travel. One usually speaks of a traditional agency (referred to as a "bricks and mortar" agency) if it primarily operates an agency or a call center for leisure travelers or an online travel agency (OTA) if sales are mostly handled online. In the business travel segment there is the travel management company, which along with operating a call center also ensures that the company's travel costs are kept under control, preferred providers are used for booking and business policies are followed. The online counterpart is the Internet TMC (ITMC) or Online TMC (OTMC).

The leisure segment usually uses an Internet Booking Engine (IBE), whereas businesses process bookings via their individually configured corporate IBE. Direct sales have increased greatly with the popularity of the Internet, so today there are almost no providers who do not also sell directly to customers. "Meta search engines"[11] and "Opaque travel sites"[12] complete the range of offers.

The graphic depicts the Information Technology systems used in the booking process. Here it can be seen that various companies (such as the GDS) constitute more than one link in the chain of value creation.

One can shop for the best rates in a number of ways using the shopping agents[13] of the GDSs or of third-party providers[14]. Quality control tools[15] ensure that a booked fare is in fact the least expensive one or is within the travel policies. The flow of money in the airline sector is handled by a clearing house[16] which collects the money from consumers and distributes it to the respective players in the travel sector.

1.2 Distribution & inventory management in detail

There is usually not a 1:1 relationship in travel distribution but rather a many to many relationship. One supplier provides its fares to many distributors, while one traveler books inventory from multiple suppliers. On a trip from Dubai to Miami, one air segment from Dubai to New York might be booked on Emirates Airlines in one inventory system while another segment is booked on American Airlines via an interline agreement[17] in a different inventory system. The rental car and hotel might again be booked in another inventory system. The booking then is referenced to as a Passenger Name Record (PNR)[18] on a GDS. To add to the complexity some of these bookings might be booked through different channels such as a direct connect interface. To find all the relevant booking records (PNRs) of one trip, it might be necessary to create a sometimes called "SuperPNR" – a combination of PNRs stored in different distribution- or inventory management systems. Before the Internet, distribution was generally handled by agencies that had access via terminal to live inventory through GDSs. These GDSs were founded by airlines to manage flight inventory. Today approximately every five years GDSs are in heavy negotiations about content and distribution fees with the airlines.

Each supplier is hosted by one of the relevant CRS providers (Sabre, Amadeus, Travelport or HP/EDS).[19] Thus, for example, Lufthansa, British Airways, Air France, United, KLM, Qantas, Iberia and many others are hosted by the Amadeus CRS. American Airlines is in the process of switching from Sabre to HP/EDS which already host Continental, US Airways and Virgin Atlantic. Sabre however recently landed JetBlue Airways. United and US Airways are hosted by the Apollo CRS which belongs to Travelport today.

The individual hosting partitions can also be seen as the suppliers' individual databases which, along with direct sales functions, communicate with the GDSs and thus use these as a distribution channel or as a global distribution system. A GDS[20] thus satisfies the demand on the market with the combined information from each supplier, no matter where it is hosted. This is possible if the GDS has a full content agreement with the respective airline.

As with the airline sector, individual reservation systems for the providers are also found in the rental car sector, in this case referred to as CRMS[21]. Thus Hertz, Avis, Alamo, EuropCar, etc. each have their own reservation system, which in turn communicates with or sends their information about consignments, prices and PNRs to the GDSs.

The structure in the hospitality sector is the same. Large hotel chains have their own reservation systems, referred to as PMS[22]. Thus, for example, there is a reservation system for the Marriot hotel chain which is used for the entire chain, i.e., for the Ritz Carlton, Marriott Hotels & Resorts, the Residence Inn by Marriot, Courtyard by Marriot and Fairfield Inn by Marriot. The same structure can be seen for Starwoods, Hilton, Hyatt, Holiday Inn, Best Western, Motel 6 and many other chains.

The same is true for the rail sector as evidenced by the Amtrak CRS, or in the ground sector as well with the reservation systems for individual taxi and limousine companies.

In the cruise sector, parent companies such as the Carnival Corporation[23], offer their subsidiaries to use the combined CRS.

The reservation systems provide many benefits and functions for each partner or level of a CRS:

1. From the perspective of the customer, the benefits are inquiries regarding products, characteristics of products, availability, prices and possibly alternative suppliers.
2. From the perspective of the travel agent, the benefits are inquiries in regards to fares, availability, information for assisting customers or sales process automation (booking documentation, invoices and payment systems).
3. For the tour operator it is used for determining capacities (remaining capacities and booking trends) as well as dynamic packaging (i.e., change packages, add transport, switch provider, or for yield management[24])
4. From the perspective of the service provider: current, medium and long-term capacity utilization, customer data (basis for Customer Relationship Management or CRM[25]), benchmarking with the competition and yield management.

Alongside the GDSs, suppliers have also recently sought opportunities for distributing their inventory via less expensive direct interfaces[26] (see Section 3.2). Once again there are consolidators[27], aggregators[28], tour operators[29] and XML technology provider who bring the various direct interfaces together[30]. The latter distribution channel can also be seen as a marketplace which in turn can be recognized as a GDSs. Furthermore, there are airlines (usually Low Cost Carriers or LCCs[31]) which are either not present at all in the GDS or do not provide all fares. Here, too, there are providers who aggregate these carriers, mostly by screen scraping[32] their websites[33].

1.3 Airline incentive model and clearing

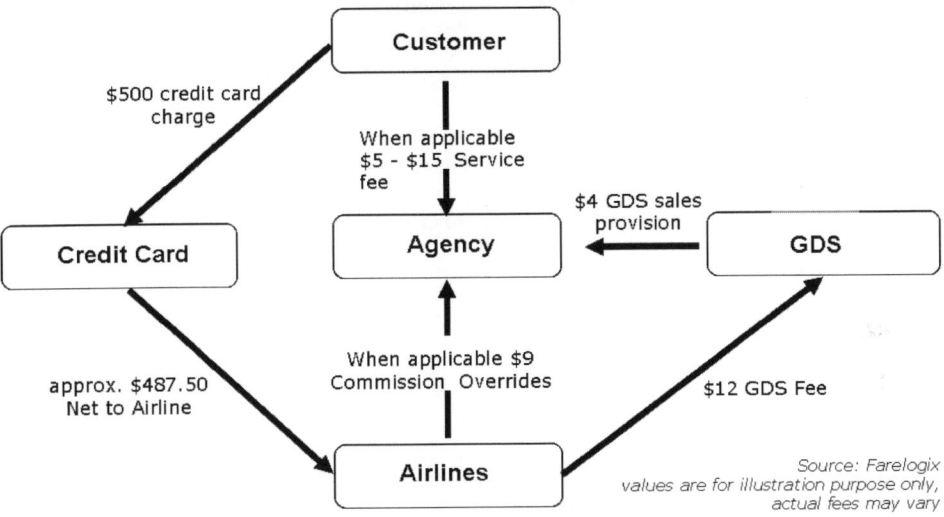

Figure 3: Airline incentive model

One model which has established itself in the airline industry is the incentive model. GDS's so-called segment fees for distribution are paid by the airline from the fee the traveler pays to it. GDSs generally pass on a part of this segment fee to the agencies who got the sale going. In some cases the agency also demands a service fee directly from the customer and in some cases also receives additional commissions directly from the airline. Part of the amount for the ticket also goes to the credit card company if payment is not made by direct debit. Therefore some airlines also apply a credit card fee. The actual distribution of the fees and commissions to the parties involved (the settlement process) is generally handled via a clearing house (such as ARC or IATA).

1.4 Figures for the travel market

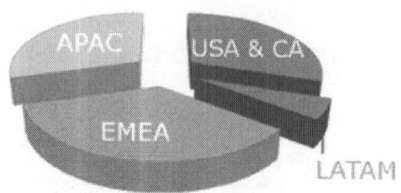

Total sum: USD 900 B
source: PhoCusWright

Figure 4: Travel market worldwide

From a worldwide perspective the North (USA and Canada) and Latin American (LatAm) market constitutes about one third, the EMEA[34] market another third and the rest of the world (APAC[35]) the last third of the world market.

Depending on the basis for observation – passengers/guests or sales – the airline or hotel sector takes the top position. In both categories the markets can be described as nearly equal in size. The overall market has a volume of about USD 900 billion per year.

Growth forecasting is currently to be enjoyed with utmost caution and virtually no research company will predict firm rates of growth. The general consensus is that the level for 2010/2011 will once again settle at that of 2006/2007. Where a decade ago the travel industry as a whole was expected to grow by 7% per year, one now assumes that growth is more likely to be around 4%.

According to PhoCusWright, the markets in Western Europe, Australia and North America are saturated, but Eastern Europe and Asia show rapid growth. South America and the Middle East also show growth in the market. Africa continues to be underdeveloped.

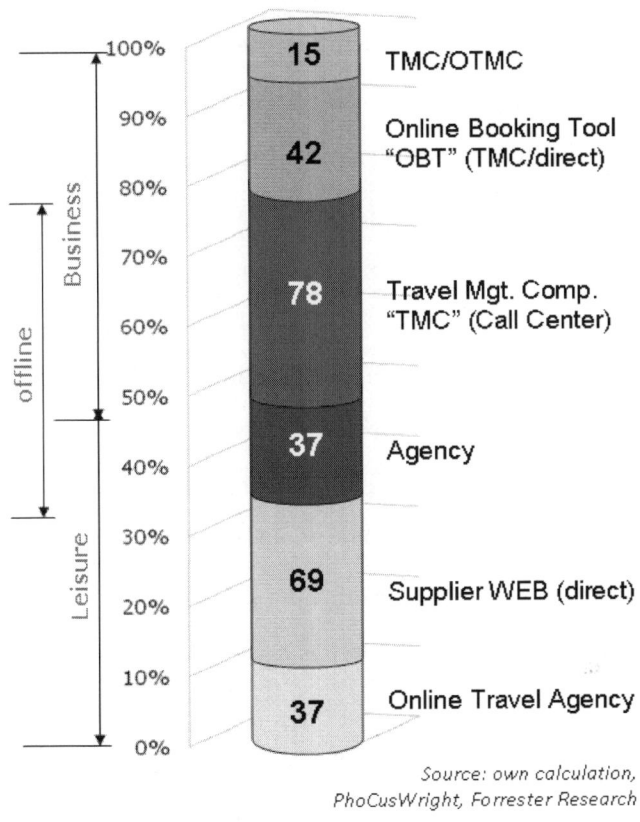

Figure 5: US Travel Market per segment

The EMEA as well as the North American markets are about the same size. The travel market consists of two large product categories: business travel and leisure travel. The leisure market makes up somewhat more than half the market in both regions[36]. Trips are either booked through a travel agency (offline or 'managed') or on the Internet (online). Online there are generally two main providers: the supplier or an online travel agency (OTA). The increasing popularity of online transactions is also seen in the travel industry. In 2010, already more than half of the bookings are being made online in EMEA as well as in North America.

1.5 History

The historical development of travel is based on human mobility. In the beginning this travel was done for practical reasons, such as the search for places with food and water and escaping from natural catastrophes, but it quickly grew to include travels for cultural reasons. In the time of the ancient Romans and Greeks, excursions to particular events, such as the Olympic Games and all manner of competitions, was a routine ritual of the rich upper class. But even pilgrimages to the temples of the gods were part of contemporary tourism, such as in ancient Egypt and other civilizations which included the hajj to Mecca or the gathering of Hindus at the Ganges River. All these popular routes as well as the economic and political power relationships with other colonies and other dependent regions and also long-distance trade supported the development of tourism infrastructure with inns and guesthouses early on. The introduction of mass transportation means such as rail and ship traffic at the beginning of the 19th century made the benefits of this mobility available to the poorer classes as well.

Introduction of information technology (IT): manual flight reservation, which was performed at the beginning of the 1970s, became too time-consuming and difficult to keep track of as supply and demand grew. With the introduction of global distribution systems, which were founded by airlines in the 1960s, travel agencies had to spend a lot of time entering reservation data manually. The airlines realized that automation of the reservation process would not only increase the productivity of travel agencies but also essentially make them an extension of the airline sales team in a sense. Consequently the GDSs have been the backbone of the online distribution system in the travel market for a long time and remain so.

Among the largest global distribution systems founded around the 1960s are:
1. Amadeus (primarily in Europe)
2. Sabre (primarily in the USA)
3. Travelport which combines:
    a. Galileo International consisting of the Apollo GDS (primarily in the USA, Mexico and Japan) and the Galileo GDS (in the remaining countries)
    b. Worldspan (primarily in the USA)

A GDS forms the basis of agency activity in the travel industry because it aggregates and manages the PNRs which it receives from the individual CRSs of the respective suppliers. It enables efficient access to capacities and current fares and deducts the capacity from the system after booking in order to avoid overbooking.

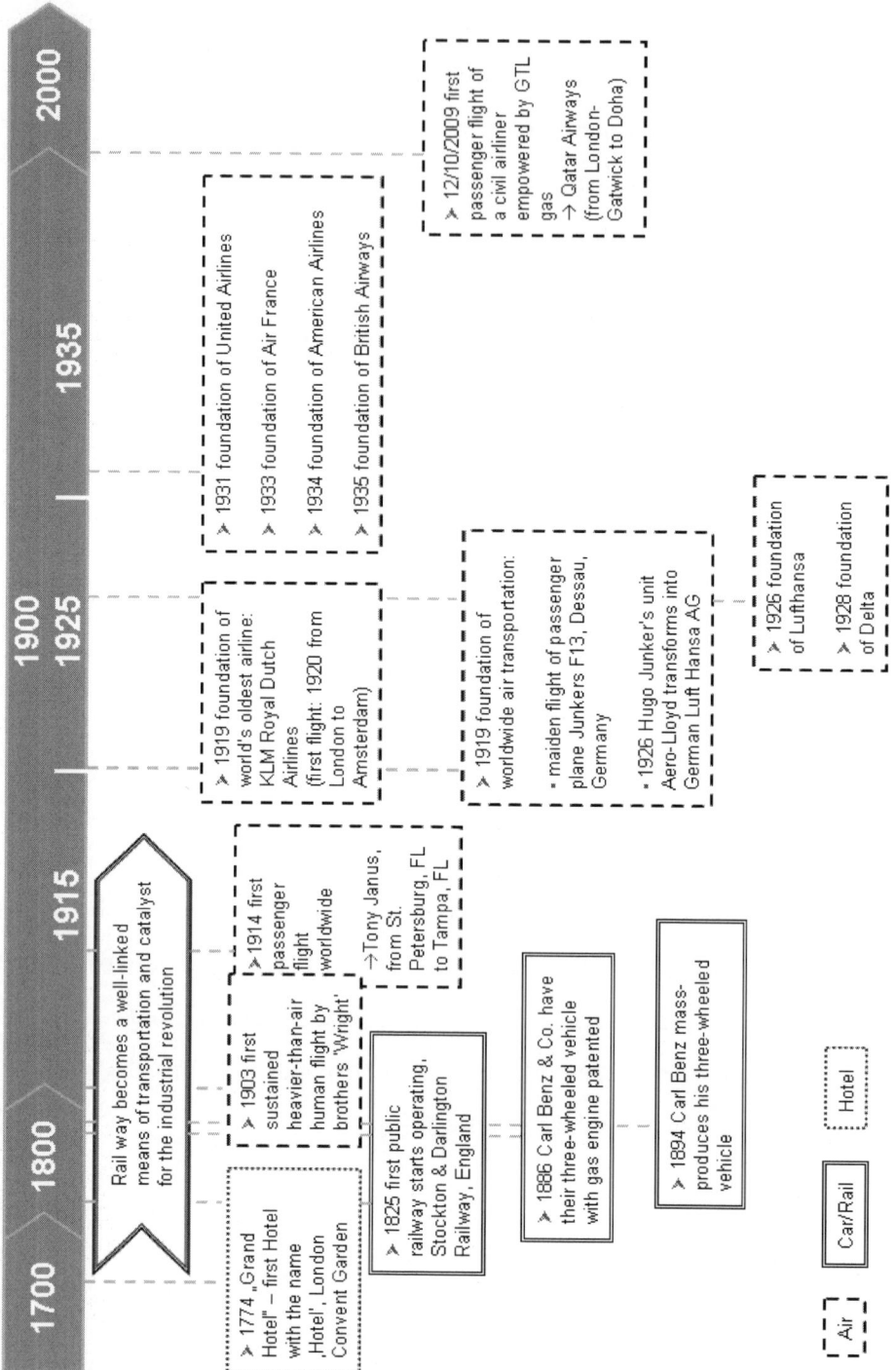

Figure 6: Suppliers' historical milestones

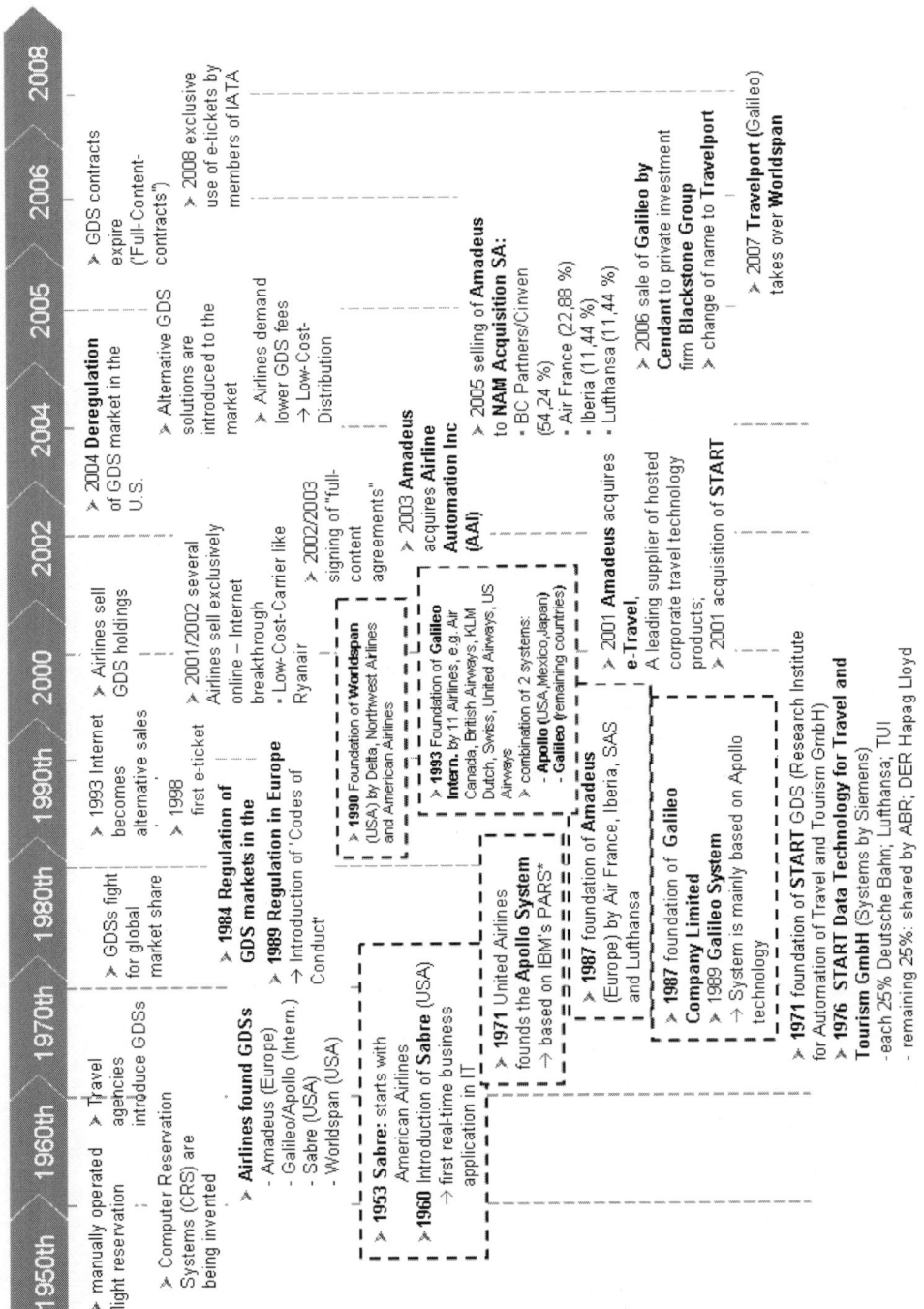

Figure 7: Suppliers' (Air) historical milestones/ Formation of GDS

Amadeus (Lufthansa, Air France, Iberia and SAS[37]) and Galileo (British Airways, KLM and Swissair) were founded by European airlines; Sabre and Worldspan developed from the internal booking systems of American Airlines, TWA[38], Delta and Northwest.[39]

After all four global distribution systems were owned by airlines, the U.S. GDS market was regulated to avoid competitive abuse in 1984. These regulations forbade preference of or discrimination against any particular airline by a GDS. For their part airlines publishing fares in the GDS were required to supply all four global distribution systems equally.

Five years later in 1989, a code of conduct was introduced to regulate the European GDS market. This code requires, among other things, that all global distribution systems be available to all airlines and travel agencies, that information not be manipulated and that airlines with shares in a GDS supply all global distribution systems with the same content.

After the American airline companies sold their shares in the global distribution systems at the end of 2000[40], the GDS market was deregulated in the US in 2004. In Europe, the code of conduct continues to apply beyond 2010[41], because Air France/KLM, Iberia and Lufthansa hold minority interests.

Since the deregulation of the GDS market in the US, airlines are free to negotiate fares with the global distribution systems and others and attempt to reduce their costs of sales in this way. This led to a change of the traditional market model in which payments flowed from the airline to the GDS (refer to Section 1.3). Now with some airlines it is sometimes the travel agencies which have to pay a booking fee to the airline (collected by the GDS) in order to get access to all fares. This method is also known as the "opt-in method"[42, 43]. As a consequence so-called "full content"[44] deals with the airlines have become a major focus in GDS/airline negotiations.

In Europe, the GDS market continues to be regulated officially[45] but presents itself as deregulated through the behavior of the parent carriers[46], which place the global distribution systems in competition with one another. This leads to a controversial view: In 2009, for example, Lufthansa, which is defined as a parent carrier[47], gave Sabre and Travelport an advantage with the introduction of preferred fares[48, 49]. The GDS Amadeus, in which Lufthansa has a minimum holding, obtained this advantage only after difficult negotiations which continued into 2010 and requires the GDS to use its own financial means in order not to lose market share. Since in this case Lufthansa is only disadvantaging its 'own' GDS, Amadeus, one view is that the European market has been deregulated for a long time or no longer requires a code of conduct, whereas other voices continue to insist that the three parent carriers should give up their shares in Amadeus entirely. It remains to be seen whether the European GDS market will now be officially deregulated as a result of this.

2 Current situation

2.1 The travel experience today

Advancing globalization and growing demand for mobility make the future of the travel industry appear secure. Even new technologies that may serve as substitutes, such as video conferences, will not replace travel. However the travel industry faces some challenges as a system, a community and as an industry: economic fluctuations, natural catastrophes, globalization, mobility, security issues and terrorist attacks, rising costs, growing demand, dependence on natural resources, the Internet and technology, aging of personnel and value creation for customers as well as employees. Each individual link in the value creation chain of the travel industry (global distribution systems, suppliers, agents, technology providers and businesses/travelers) should be aware of its responsibility with respect to the innovation process and be open to a change in which all parties work together on solutions in order to meet the continuously growing challenges.

If one compares the innovative drive with other industries such as telecommunications, one notes that customers barely experience innovation directly on their flights. Ten years ago a traveler might have boarded a Boeing 737 packing a heavy mobile telephone. Today the same traveler will board a similar Boeing 737 offering much less service but with a smartphone in hand that can not only make calls but also take pictures, play music and films, manage e-mail, surf the Internet and play games, at least while still on the ground. The telecommunications industry has caught up to the strengths of the aviation sector, for example in establishing international standards (See Section 1.4) with the introduction of mobile telephone networks operating worldwide. As the following sections show, great potential for innovation in the travel sector remains.

One trend started by the no-frills airlines is to make fares appear cheaper at first glance by dividing up the individual cost items differently. In the travel industry, this method is referred to as "unbundling"[50] (See Section 2.5). Thus unbundling leads to the paradoxical situation that although many customers can perform price comparisons more easily than ever through the use of the Internet and new technologies, these fares come with less service. Therefore the online customer must read the fine print in order to keep an overview of the complexity of unbundled fares. Previously, customers could depend on travel agencies or third-party providers. Today, price comparisons of available flights and booking them can be handled without a travel agency. However the complexity now associated with the services included in a fare or not make such comparisons increasingly difficult. Components, such as booking restrictions and essentials which are important to the individual traveler, must be part of a serious price comparison. In the future individual preferences may vary however: one person might prefer a pillow and blanket while others prefer a guaranteed overhead bin space. This is why customers are once again glad to have this task handled by others.

Particularly in the European and American markets, agencies often still work with computer programs characterized by cryptic commands and archaic interfaces. This points to a lack of enthusiasm for innovation, but it is also a challenge to be met by IT, because even modern systems with graphical user interfaces must allow efficient operation using only the keyboard and no mouse. The increase in the average age of employees also underscores this: according to a study by the market research firm PhoCusWright, in 2008 about 80 percent of employees in US travel agencies were over 45 years of age. How will this situation look in 2020? A clear dividing line between the generations can be seen: while experienced agents accomplish tasks efficiently with a cryptic screen, younger colleagues who grew up with digital media, cell phones and social networks perform significantly better with graphical media. Another aspect not to be underestimated is that cryptic screens are limited to 64 characters per line and require additional pages ("move-downs") of the display for less relevant information. This fact limits in particular the display of special add-on services (see Section 3.6). A "picture" really can say more than a thousand cryptic characters[51].

Innovations tend to be viewed critically or even blocked. Openness and cooperation are rare. It is apparent that some market participants in the travel industry pursue a strategy of defending obsolete systems, business models and processes. Clinging to what is claimed to be 'proven' can have a somewhat inhibitory effect on innovation. Shouldn't leading market players drive technologies forward instead of being driven by them? (See section 4)

One aspect which should not be forgotten is that developing countries could pursue a targeted entry strategy in the sector by exploiting the lack of innovation on the part of developed countries. While agents in developed countries continue to work with cryptic commands, in countries such as India, China and Russia, agencies embrace graphical user interfaces with enthusiasm. Possible consequences are outlined in Section 5. Other sectors have experienced this already. Computers and cell phones, for example, are manufactured mostly in Asian countries these days. Thus several western domains have suddenly become a driving force for Asian trade. In the travel industry, an example are call centers located in India. These call centers operate in the name of global companies. It is easy for companies in developing nations to engage in medium-term established businesses in developed nations (equity joint ventures), particularly because they already use new technologies and are not shy about investing in innovations. This factor is reinforced by a strong domestic market: China (1.3 billion inhabitants) and India (1.2 billion inhabitants) will inevitably eclipse the travel offerings of the US (310 million inhabitants) or the most populous European country (Germany with 82 million inhabitants). Systems established in India or China based on the latest technologies can also prevail in developed nations in the medium term.

The current sales situation is characterized by increased competition due to conflicts of interest. The strategy in the business sector, i.e., that of TMCs, consists of integrating all the content of various global distribution systems, low-cost carriers, etc. and controlling the travel market online as well as offline. However, there is a great shortcoming with regard to the greater innovation needed to avoid dependence on global distribution systems. This is because the TMCs increasingly compete with other market participants to whom the online business segment also appears profitable. Whereas on one hand large TMCs represent a noteworthy international sales channel for the makers of booking engines, it must not be forgotten that these producers (including, among others, global distribution systems) could also sell their booking tools directly to large companies. This strategy of disintermediation is widespread in the sector and continually leads to new conflicts of interest and increased competition. Circumventing the middleman is currently a favored adaptation strategy for nearly all market participants in order to respond to changes in the market or to tide themselves over in crises, because costs can be saved. More on this will be found in Section 2.4.

2.2 Strengths

The strengths of the travel industry lie in global organization and the definition of uniform standards. The worldwide network of global distribution systems, which integrates various internationally located providers in a uniform working interface, reflects the global organization of the travel industry.

The definition of global standards, such as unique airport- and airline codes, represents a great advantage for the travel industry. If one compares this, for example, with bank applications, which differ in every country or even with the non-standardized network systems of telephone providers in different countries, the unambiguously beneficial factor in the travel industry becomes clearly apparent in contrast with these other industries. Even in the telecommunications industry, GSM - a global mobile phone standard - became a worldwide success and eclipsed competing standards such as CDMA and TDMA because it was an open standard and network operators, end device manufacturers and technology providers worked together despite competition.

In the globalized world, along with consumer travel, regular business trips for regionally active managers are indispensable. According to an Oxford Economics study[52] managers and business travelers are convinced that about 28 percent of ongoing business would be lost without personal meetings. Personal meetings lead to about 40 percent of prospects becoming new customers compared to a conversion of just 16 percent without. Furthermore, the study showed that a personal meeting with a customer generated an average of USD 15.00 to 20.00 return for every dollar invested.

2.3 Weaknesses

Along with the travel industry's particular susceptibility to crises (9/11, SARS, swine flu and the financial crisis, for example) suppliers become very creative in finding new revenue streams by selling pillows, seat assignments, even luggage space in your overhead bin, etc., prompting comedians to join the fun (commenting on bathroom usage fees or extra charges for a seat belt).

Technology providers focus more on explaining limitations of their technology instead of its abilities and most times the productivity of agents is measured in call handling time instead of their ability to consult the traveler. One scarcely hears that the passenger, the consumer, is the central concern. All too often this is obscured by the battle for his business and the search for corresponding strategies of success.

2.4 The necessary change – innovation and quality

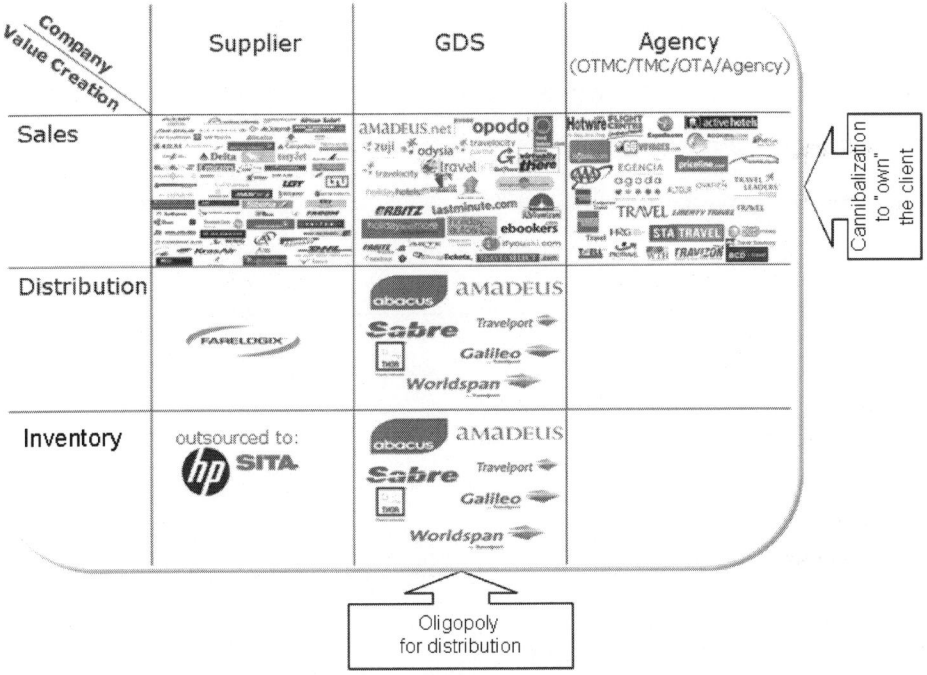

Figure 6: Players in the value creation segment

The illustration shows which companies are active in which segment of the value chain: The rows represent the added value (supplier inventory, distribution and sales); the columns indicate which companies are represented by what subsidiaries in the various areas of value creation. The table highlights the cannibalistic nature of the current market: airlines attempt to distribute directly and circumvent the GDSs; GDSs make booking tools available to agencies and TMCs while at the same time operating their own OTAs and OTMCs and thus competing directly with agencies. Moreover, GDSs control which technology companies are granted access and which are not, while the US Department of Justice must review this situation in individual cases time and again.

From the number of companies one can draw conclusions regarding how many are concentrated in a particular market segment and how fierce the competition in this segment is. Ideally, each company focuses on what it does best. In other words the supplier manages its inventory, the GDS ensures worldwide distribution and an agency provides its consulting and sales services to the market (businesses and consumers).

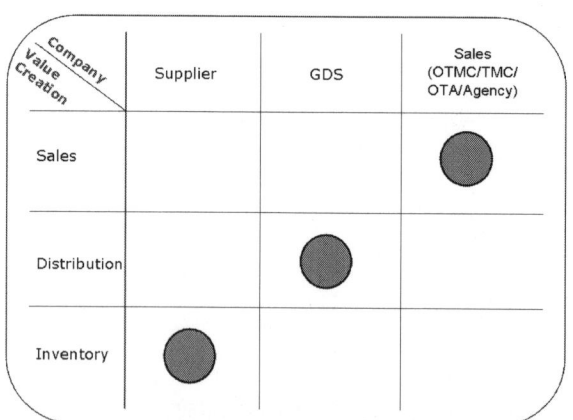

Figure 7: Classical representation of players

The illustration displays the basic idea of the travel value chain and its fulfillment. Each party focuses on the segment it handles best.

The actual landscape, on the other hand indicates a clear overemphasis on global distribution systems, enabling them to play a predominant role in the market almost like an oligopoly. Furthermore, there is a concentration in sales, which is an area of fierce competition among suppliers themselves, GDSs, agencies and TMCs.

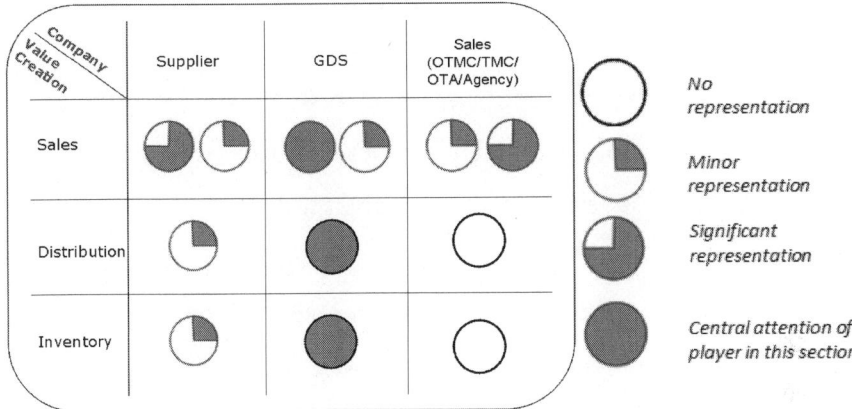

Figure 8: Current representation of players

This illustration displays the actual state of affairs of the travel value chain. The sales field shows a highly elevated concentration of competitors. This along with the barrier in the GDS column points out the GDSs' position of power.

The bottom line is that travelers and businesses pay a significant amount for GDS distribution which modern technology firms claim to be able to offer at a fraction of that cost.

> **PROTECTIONISM AND COMPETITION:**
>
> Examples from other fields show that protectionism with regard to data is not legitimate. It is considered a misuse of a dominant market position, for example, if the controlling position on the market for operating systems is abused by creating compatibility problems in order to take over related markets. In Germany, a company is considered to have a dominant market position if its market share constitutes one third.
>
> The question of abuse by refusing to disclose interfaces was already discussed at the beginning of the 1980s. At that time, IBM introduced System/370 and refused to disclose the interfaces required for developing complementary auxiliary equipment. This was seen as an abusive obstruction of competition by IBM. This was a formative case for the prevalent understanding in Europe that the owner of an industry standard cannot simply reserve the related hardware and software markets for itself.
>
> In July 2000, the European Commission classified as abusive Microsoft's refusal to give its competitor Sun the information necessary to design workgroup server operating systems which can communicate seamlessly with the "Active Directory domain architecture".
>
> Linking the sale of a product to another product earned Microsoft a fine of € 497 million when Windows Media Player was integrated as a standard part of its operating system.

Airlines, which are always subject to financial pressure, are attempting to break up established structures with new strategies (See Section 3.2 and 3.5) but are finding the GDSs to be extremely powerful opponents who also have the financial resources to wage price wars (for example, Amadeus matched Lufthansa's preferred fares program in 2009) or isolate themselves successfully (for example, Sabre terminated their agreement with Farelogix in 2009 forcing them to rethink their strategy) until the ambitious innovator runs out of steam, investors withdraw or the competition steals the show from the troublemaker who wants to impose a new order. Other players on the market merge or acquire assets (for example, Travelport acquired assets from G2switchworks in 2008) and thus eliminate competition.

In these hard-fought markets, participants often think of only first-order[53] solutions: defend and build walls. Second-order solutions would often accomplish the goals better if the concern is to secure and expand market share. Market participants can hardly behave effectively in such a market environment. The consequence is a dearth of innovation, because the actions of each are focused only on quarterly results. Few attempt to plan long-term investments for innovation. The technology providers and trendsetters and the main players in the market (suppliers, distributors and sellers) are faced with a special problem. They develop something and soon afterwards, the parties have come to an agreement and the product is no longer needed, or the customer is prevented from using it in some other way. The few modern applications are slapped together in more of a quick and dirty manner than one reflecting a clear strategy for quality. The technological potentials remain untapped (See section 4.5).[54]

The travel industry interprets the term "innovation" as the solution to the question of how to cope more efficiently with greater volume or more (passenger) traffic and how these could be expanded further. But the introduction of new technologies is left to the last possible moment prior to disasters. Shouldn't innovations be focused more on creating added value for the customer and thus improving market position through customer satisfaction?

Moore's Law[55] predicts that users can double their information technology "experience" every two years. Groundbreaking technological innovations would enable one to satisfy the expectations of travelers in accordance with Moore's Law. But are there such innovations in the travel industry?

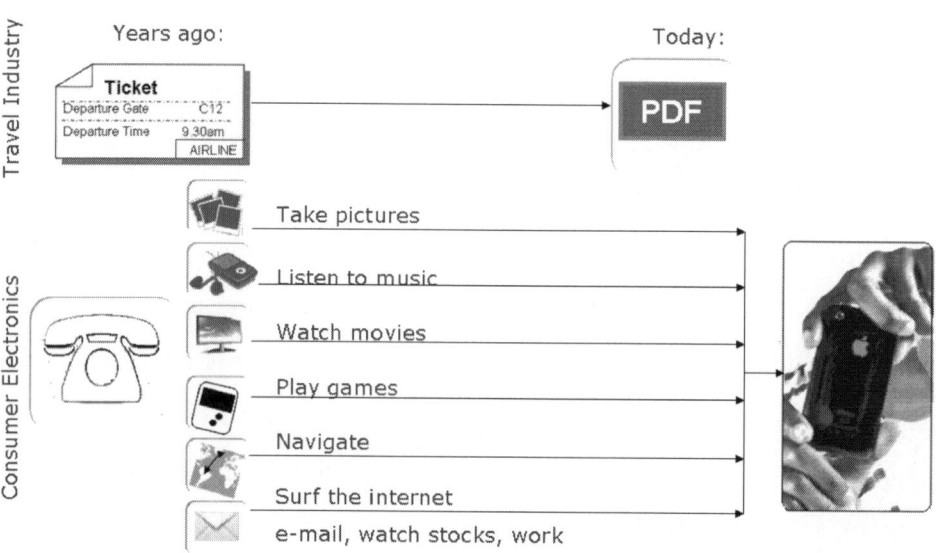

Figure 9: Innovation check of travel compared to other industries

Some incumbents interpret the introduction of the e-ticket as an innovation. Some airlines at least offer the ticket on mobile telephones. The search for specialized trips (such as shopping agents for diving vacations, study trips or where one can travel with a certain amount of money) is also called "innovation". However, this is viewed with some controversy: In the same period, other industries have linked all aspects of entertainment to the mobile office with permanent availability in a format small enough to fit in our pockets. A 2010 report[56] by PhoCusWright states that airlines are particularly irritated by the inefficiency and inflexibility of GDSs and are therefore looking for options to circumvent them altogether. Thus, for example, the sale of additional services (see Section 3.5) at airlines – an area of business where airlines hope to make 30% of their sales in the future – was implemented in mere months on airline websites but took significantly longer in the GDS channel.

Conventional definitions of the term "innovation" are, for example:
1. incremental, radical and revolutionary changes in thinking, products, processes or organizations
2. producing something new and significantly different from the old; and
3. a change that significantly increases added value for customers or producers.

One is led to suspect that ordinary progress takes place in the travel industry, but actual innovation appears to be controversial at the least. The goal of an innovation is to make a positive change in order to improve something. The various interpretations of the term "innovation" suggest strongly that the travel industry does enjoy regular, ongoing technological progress which however is rarely accompanied by innovation.

2.5 Challenges

Challenges in the travel industry are constituted by the established boundaries, which must be crossed. Boundaries usually result in the grouping of members, from which cultural groups are developed in turn.

Members of a cultural group have a strong relationship to their group, as the group and its members are believed to share the same or a similar culture. The reflexivity of the group, i.e., the feedback which members of the group provide to each other decreases as new approaches to processes, systems, solutions and innovations are not fostered in a closed system. In extreme cases, with a severe lack of feedback, this can mean that the group ends up with a distorted view of reality thinking they do everything right, while those outside the group do everything wrong.

A group takes on established goals in order to work **with** them, but not to work **on** them. This destroys their flexibility in shaping goals as well as eliminates innovation in and change to these goals. Processes do not continue to be developed and become obsolete; opportunities are overlooked and fast responses to the constantly changing environment are impossible. Innovations cannot take place, as innovative ideas are lost due to the stable alignment within the group. However, a market requires flexible boundaries in order to be effective.[57]

The financial system behaved like such a closed system until 2008 - hardly anyone looked at it critically, everyone wanted to ride the wave, and those who voiced criticism were ignored, defamed or drowned out.

The travel industry likewise shows clear signs of being a closed system: Based on first-order solutions, the system is marking time and trying to stabilize itself. Criticism is re-interpreted and perceptions appear distorted, although much greater demands will be made of the industry in future (See section 3.5). With the exception of direct distribution, distribution will be divided among three large GDSs throughout large parts of the world. Agreements even include penalty fees if a portion of a trip is booked elsewhere. Some say the travel industry is in a downward spiral. A revolution is becoming increasingly likely. With such severe restrictions, no change can take place - unless it comes from outside. A rigid system is subjected to increasing pressure until it can no longer compensate and the limits of the system are demolished as if by a revolution.

The aforementioned arguments indicate that this is also a current threat to the travel industry. However, if the system succeeds in expanding its limits, it can make positive use of the existing opportunities. Change must be viewed positively and criticism fostered. Only those who change steadily and consistently will remain ahead of the game. Nokia transformed itself from a rubber boot producer to the world's largest mobile phone manufacturer. Where would Apple be today if it did not constantly change its product portfolio? The travel industry has the perfect initial situation and can benefit from practically all innovations outside the sector (see Trends, Section 3).

2.6 Opportunities

According to organizational behavior theory,[58] an entire system is closed when there are boundaries and there is almost no exchange of ideas or stimuli from the outside. On the other hand, the best output can be achieved if there is a cooperative culture that links the participants, all of whom want to achieve the same objective. Thus the market as a whole can achieve the common goal of providing a better experience for travelers.[59] Furthermore, there should be a network culture in which each member should be able to express himself freely without fearing the consequences.[60]

Open boundaries are essential to success in a changing environment. Initially, this can lead to uncertainty, as the old, established corporate culture, which may give its members a strong sense of identification, is broken up. At first glance, it may appear that security and prosperity are being lost. However, according to organizational behavior theory, effectivity increases the more the group drifts apart, moves out of its comfort zone and approaches new, unexplored terrain. Freedom of opinion promotes the expression of constructive criticism.[61] Groups which engage in reciprocal review or express constructive criticism do not perceive principles as givens but rather as restrictions to be manipulated, not limits within which they must work.[62] To this extent the following trends are to be seen as opportunities for the system, not as threats.

3 Trends

3.1 Cell phones / Mobiles

Of all communications instruments, mobile telephones, in this document referred to as "cell phones", are the most widespread and they are taken everywhere. According to Forrester Research, more than 80% of the population in North America own a cell phone. Almost the same number are online as well[63]. Three quarters of households also have a broadband connection. The figures are similar for other industrialized nations. In weaker economic regions around the world, the cell phone is usually the first point of access to the Internet due to lack of regular land lines. Twice as many people use Short Message Service (SMS) as e-mail. Due to Apple, Research in Motion and Google, among others, the Smartphone is now predominant in most western countries. Apple's iPhone Store offers well over 14,000 travel applications from a network of more than 245,000[64] currently available applications overall.

Travelers in particular depend on their mobile devices so they can be reached at all times and so that they can retrieve information immediately. According to Forrester, 93% of all American flight passengers are online. Of these, 51% are younger than 43 and thus even more technologically inclined.

The topic of travel bookings has a special position in the top ten things people do with their mobile devices: while most activities in the top 10 have to do with information procurement on the go, travel applications can be used interactively or can be designed to be semi-automated based on rules.

According to Forrester, business travelers already want to shift tasks from their desks to their cell phones. At the latest at the point when the human-machine interface is improved even more or cell phones are able to project images, comparable developments will be implemented on a massive scale.

The mere number of available applications is no guarantee for success, as the initial interest in an application quickly vanishes if the service is not good and fails to simplify daily life. What good is it if you can check your flight departure time on 2000 applications? It is better if providers focus on core services, program them successfully, and make them available to other providers. In the medium term, travelers will want to use a travel application that offers a range of different features. Here as well, the marketplace philosophy will take over, as with Amazon, which offers third-party features as well as its own.

Consumer behavior will probably change drastically: people will board a plane without having a confirmed hotel reservation at their destination, as they will take care of this on the way there (or while still on the ground). At the PhoCusWright Travel Innovation Summit Conference in Orlando, Florida in autumn 2009, there was even talk of mobile devices being responsible for the fastest transition in the travel industry in history: the cell phone would be the primary point of sale for goods and services additionally sold after bookings. (The technical term for this is "post-booking merchandising"; see Section 3.5). Restaurants at the airport or on the way from the destination airport to the hotel will market their services to travelers - targeted advertising that will assist travelers instead of annoying them, facilitated by location-dependent services such as GPS[65]. Although users will probably not book their vacations via their cell phones, business and leisure travelers will make additional bookings and rebookings and search for information when their plans change. New devices such as Apple's iPad or devices not yet known today can certainly become the entry point for travelers. If calendar functions as well as GPS and Geo data are included, the applications are limitless (See section 3.7). The general consensus is that just as the Internet revolutionized travel bookings, the cell phone triggers a new wave of changes.

As a rule, in the medium term only a healthy combination of mobile application, online application and personal service will prevail. The mobile application will have to implement the benefits of mobility (time and location-dependent services as well as rule-based support) and must not be merely a mirror image of the online application. For example, such a service should recognize that you're still in a meeting in Miami Beach at 11:00 a.m. (time/location information), note that an accident has occurred on the I-95 going north (event/traffic info) and that it is therefore impossible to make the flight from Fort Lauderdale to La Guardia at 2:00 p.m. (route planning). The application therefore automatically finds an alternate flight from Miami to JFK Airport that leaves at 2:30 p.m. Thus you even have an extra half hour's time in the office. If this is OK, you confirm it with one click and the alternative would be booked, an aisle seat reserved as desired, the appointment for dinner in Port Chester informed of the dinner being postponed by an hour and the "exchange"[66] carried out. In the background the travel policies would already have been reviewed and approved (or an approval process initiated). The rental car would likewise be rebooked and the required navigation points sent to the cell phone so that you can check the new route during the flight (offline, if necessary). The restaurant, assuming it doesn't (yet) have an online reservation interface, would be informed of the delayed dinner reservation via an intuitive automated voice service. Should the restaurant be unable to approve the change, you would be connected with the restaurant receptionist to clarify the issue. Should one of your partners be unable to confirm the delayed appointment, the application offers the option to initiate a connection so that a direct telephone call can be made. The further possibilities are endless: automatic request to leave now (order a taxi or take your own car, depending on whether the taxi or parking is cheaper), automatic check-in, navigation to the baggage drop and fee payment, avoidance of lines at security checkpoints, an application that knows where the travelers are located, guides them efficiently through the gates depending on how quickly they have to depart, board the aircraft using RFID[67], etc. All of the services could also be equipped with an intuitive voice recognition system.

But even this example shows that innovation within the travel industry is partially dependent on innovations in other sectors (in this case, telecommunications). The adaptation of innovations from other sectors is a first step – the industry would do better to offer its own innovations as well.

3.2 Direct distribution

Increasing numbers of commercial air carriers consider high distribution fees to be a thorn in their sides.

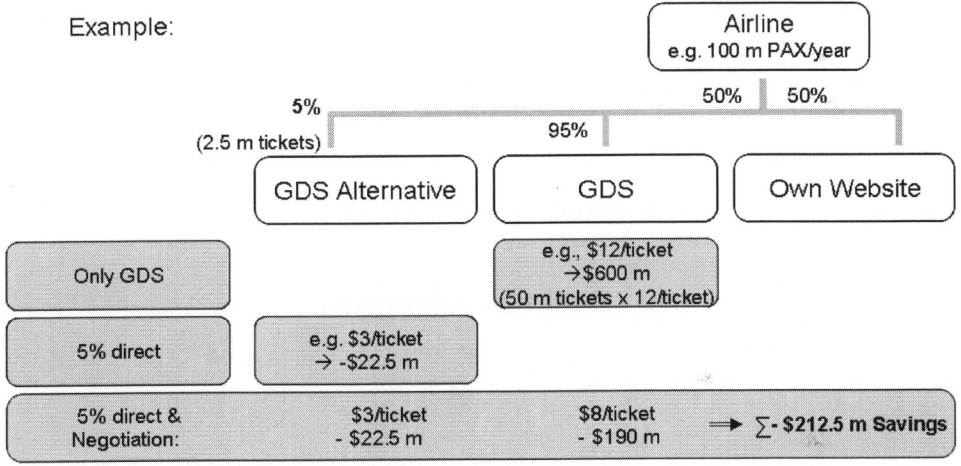

Figure 10: Direct distribution supplier savings

Assume that an airline pays USD 12.00 per booking to the GDS while it pays only USD 3.00 to an alternative provider. In this example, the airline handles 100 million passengers each year and processes 50% of the bookings directly, most likely via their own website. This leaves 50 million that are processed by the GDS. That means USD 600 million in fees. If the airline were to move 5% of this volume to alternative channels, USD 22.5 million would be saved. On the other hand, its negotiating position vis-à-vis the GDSs would be much better and certainly USD 12.00 can be much more easily reduced to USD 8.00 per booking given the GDS's risk of losing their entire business. Based on this example, actively supporting an alternative provider would mean the airline could save over USD 200 million per year - while the alternative provider would receive USD 7.5 million in financing annually - a considerable sum for start-ups – and this is just one airline considered.

That means that while low-cost carriers (LCCs) are increasingly maneuvering their inventory to the inventory unit of the GDSs (easyjet, Jetblue, Westjet), major airlines are trying to exert more control over their distribution actively influencing the distribution unit of the GDSs. This again highlights the logic and importance of separating inventory management and distribution. See also Section 5.2.

3.3 Virtual meetings / Video conferences

Due to the global economic crisis as well as the swine flu pandemic, there was a significant increase in video conferences as alternatives to business trips in 2009. Video images in poor resolution jerking across a screen must be avoided and user-friendliness significantly increased if the providers want to make their video-conferencing solutions more attractive and thus more marketable.

Personal meetings are indisputably the key to the success of business relationships. Likewise, personal encounters play a significant role in finalizing deals. On the other hand, many wish to deal with their suppliers on a virtual basis. Assuming everyone is either a client or a provider, there is an obvious conflict that must be resolved in the medium term.

A further aspect is a simple calculation: a salesperson is generally judged by his figures. For example, if he has a closing rate of 5% and finds out that this is halved by virtual meetings, but that he can conduct five times[68] as many meetings in the same period, he will more than double his result at the end of the month[69].

Virtual client presentations[70] and Webinars already have a significant influence on the sales process today. It used to be extremely difficult to plan a joint meeting between sellers and buyers of large multinational enterprises, when experts located in different regions should all get together. Today the setup of an online meeting is a walk in the park.

Of course, one must not forget to take cultural differences into account from a global standpoint. In the emerging economies in Asia and in the Middle East as well, personal meetings are essential in maintaining customer relationships.

In summary, one can say that the weekly on-site get-together will fall victim to redlining, while personal meetings are necessary to seal the beginning of a business relationship, to clarify important issues and conclude deals as well as to maintain good customer relationships.

3.4 Going green

In addition to business continuity aspects that enable the business to continue to operate regardless of location, even during a pandemic, carbon dioxide emissions play an increasingly important role for many people.

Airlines usually like to tailor their image so as to present airplanes as the safest and most environmentally friendly form of travel.

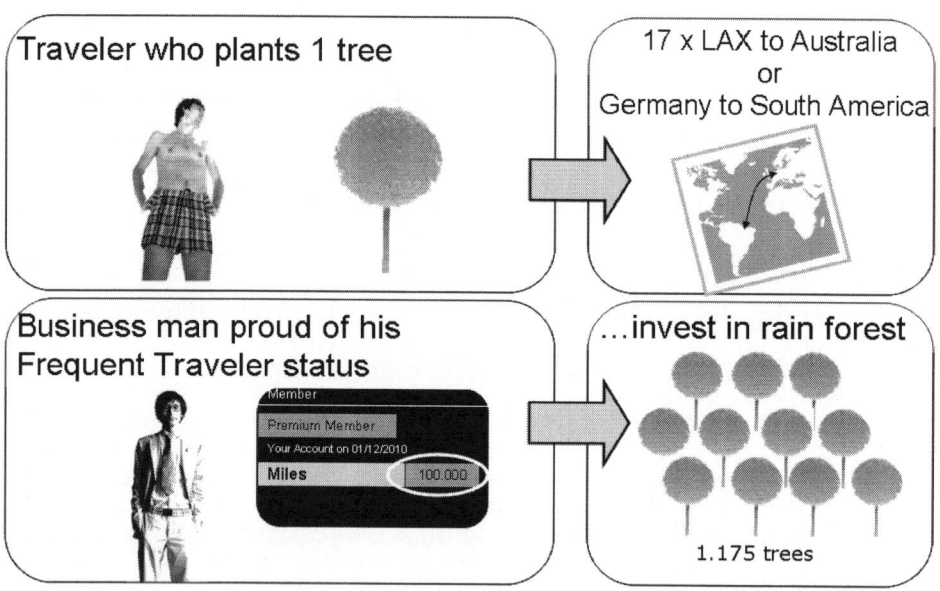

Figure 11: Carbon dioxide offset requirements

However, reality is different. A tourist who thinks about whether it is environmentally friendly to fly to Australia for one month once in his lifetime, but simultaneously plants a tree in his garden at home, can make the journey almost every second year and has made his contribution to the environment.[71] On the other hand, a business traveler who boasts of putting 100,000 miles per year on his frequent flyer account is another story. Such a traveler would have to plant a forest with 1,175 trees to compensate for all the emissions.

Increasingly, environmentally friendly tour operators are appearing who plan minimum distances for flights and minimum stays and who do not offer any off-road tours or sightseeing flights. Such tour operators generally offer to pay a voluntary CO_2 emissions fee as well. This is usually incorporated in contemporary IT systems.

Another popular tool of sustainable tourism is the voluntary climate protection contribution paid by the customers. Depending on the level of CO_2 emissions, which is determined using an emissions calculator, a certain fee is due. Travelers can donate this amount on a voluntary basis. These revenues are used in turn for solar, hydropower, biomass and energy-saving projects.

The idea of ecological responsibility is spreading throughout the entire travel industry and is being adopted by more and more operators and even airline companies. For example, Lufthansa now includes voluntary customer climate protection contributions in its offers and the German operators of Thomas Cook AG[72] (Neckermann Reisen, Thomas Cook Reisen, Bucher Last Minute) have offered the voluntary climate protection donation to customers since 2008.

The demand for Corporate Social Responsibility (CSR)[73] is also increasing in the hospitality sector. Thus, for instance, the Rezidor hotel chain (Radisson, Regent International, Park Inn) with 272 hotels around the globe offers a loyalty program with which the customers can compensate for the emissions produced by the hotels by donating their loyalty points. With these proceeds, Rezidor supports energy conservation projects worldwide. The commitment to nature is also manifested in a variety of local projects and programs.[74] For instance, the Radisson Blu Hotel in Berlin carried out a "Clean-up Day" in the local area and the Haus am Schloss Fleesensee immersed the castle in candlelight for an hour during the "Lights Out" project.

Active eco-marketing has become an integral part of CSR for rental car companies as well. For example, Hertz offers its customers more than 1500 low-emission cars and has already added 400 hybrids to its fleet[75]. Its competitor Avis calls itself the first climate-neutral car rental company in the world using the slogan "CO_2 Neutral". Together with The Carbon Neutral Company, a leading environmental protection organization in Europe, Avis has already planted over 200,000 trees, thus helping to neutralize CO_2 emissions to counteract the greenhouse effect.[76]

Whether these projects largely contribute to effective climate protection or merely constitute an ingenious marketing strategy is up for debate - but despite the blurry boundaries between active environmental protection and eco-marketing, the public's awareness of responsibility for climate protection has been raised, along with an awareness that something will and must change.

Air traffic contributes to the greenhouse effect via numerous pollutants and various effects. Its share of the overall manmade greenhouse effect is currently estimated at 9 %[77].

Particularly in the age of globalization, the growth figures of the international travel market are reflected. While the less harmful rail and road traffic is declining as a percentage of travel traffic overall, according to the market research company GfK[78], based in Germany, air traffic increased by 6 percent (excluding business travel!) between 1996 and 2008.

3.5 Ancillary fees via merchandising

Ancillary revenues are revenues introduced in the US in 2008/9 by almost all major airlines following the example of profitable low-cost carriers. Passengers pay extra for services which were previously included in the fares. An example of this is the baggage fee. In 2008 airlines had already earned more than USD 10.25 billion with ancillary revenues (up from USD 2.29 billion in 2006)[79]. Currently, many airlines are thus obtaining approximately 4% of their operative income from ancillary fees.[80] Several of the largest airlines expect to earn 30%-40% of their sales from ancillary fees by 2014. How is this possible? A one-way flight from Miami to Chicago is available for USD 83.00. However, if you wish to check 2 pieces of luggage, reserve a seat in advance, possibly with more leg space or at an emergency exit, you will pay extra. Meals are no longer included either, and even non-alcoholic drinks may soon cost extra. Some airlines even charge fees for a blanket or a pillow. If you then wish to work in the lounge in peace or even manage to get on an earlier flight, an extra charge in the range of the price of the original ticket is also due. Thus, for various flights 60% - 70% of revenues may be earned via ancillary fees. As previously mentioned in Section 3.1 the cell phone will play a significant role in booking these additional service fees. Furthermore, cell phones are personalized with their owners' preferences, so that applications can be developed which will sell travelers exactly what they want.

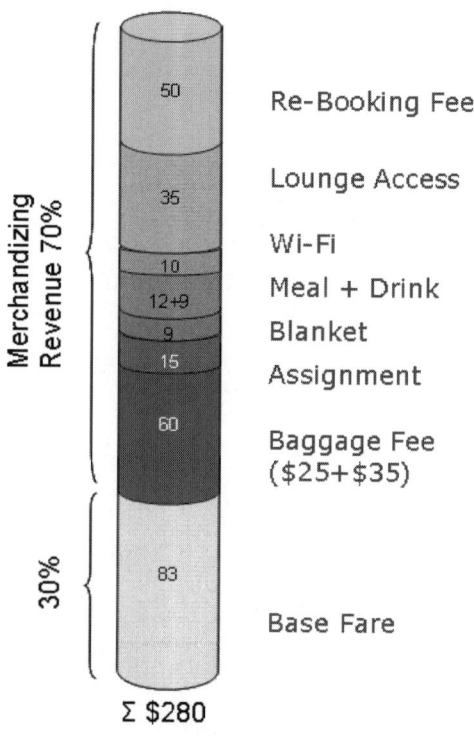

Figure 12: Ancillary Revenue (airlines)

According to Forrester Research, 43% of passengers want a guaranteed space for their carry-on bags in the overhead bins, 24% wish to wait less than 10 minutes at the security checkpoints, 26% want to be able to pick up their baggage faster, and 20% want electrical outlets at their seat so they can work during flights. Another 38% do not want to sit near families with children. One might not to want to publically admit the latter, but might well pay for it. Seat reservations are definitely one way of earning extra money. According to a survey by USA Today[81], 61% of passengers prefer window seats, 38% prefer aisle seats, and why 1% prefers seats in the middle is anybody's guess. These are all challenges that future systems need to meet.

Loyalty programs based solely on miles will no longer be sufficient in the future: a traveler who books the aforementioned fare but rebooks twice, checks luggage and uses additional services rapidly becomes a "valuable" guest spending around USD 300 for this trip. If the traveler paying USD 300 is now seated in a middle row next to one who has only paid the cheapest fare, brought his own food and has not made any additional purchases but has the favored window seat, problems are bound to arise if these two exchange information. The airline should avoid this, particularly in view of the fact that such experiences are also transmitted to the public via social networks (Section 3.6). On the other hand, this means that all possible systems and personnel that the traveler could come in contact with need to be informed of the value of the guest for preferred treatment. This includes the online application, the mobile application, the travel agency, the ground staff, as well as the cabin crew. This is an enormous demand being made of IT.

Merchandising is defined as the maximization of sales of goods with the aid of product design, selection, packaging, pricing and presentation that stimulates consumers to spend more. As already mentioned in Section 2.4, cryptic screens are not suited to selling ancillary services. According to Air Canada and Farelogix, that would be like supermarket chains arranging breakfast cereals sideways for storage reasons, even though the manufacturers spend enormous amounts of money to differentiate themselves from the competition with their packaging.

Particularly with regard to flight, differentiation by brand is one of the most important criteria for the future. A seat is always just a seat, but there are significant differences between sitting in a Mercedes, Porsche, Audi or a BMW. As supply increases, the airlines must also achieve this sort of differentiation.

Ancillary fees could be considered one of the major innovations in 2008/2009. Even if they don't provide any genuine customer benefit, according to the definition in Section 2.4, they could be regarded as an approach to innovation, as they represent a revolutionary change and increase the worth of the manufacturer. However, ancillary fees are not truly substantively new.

A number of companies in the industry have undertaken technical developments so that ancillary fees can be invoiced. This was facilitated by the Electronic Miscellaneous Document (EMD)[82] in mid-2010. Eventually EMDs will replace MCOs (Miscellaneous Charge Orders). Originally, IATA had wanted to wait until the airlines had agreed on a standard for bank settlements in 2012.

The GDSs suffered a setback when they wanted a share of the fees for luggage and pillows. Up to 50% was suggested, but the airlines clearly had a different agenda. TMCs initially saw no added value for themselves in selling their customers ancillary services and thus expected that their agents would not be much inclined to sell features without receiving any of the proceeds. How is a TMC agent supposed to explain to a traveler that five extra transactions were just carried out and that the service fee will have to be raised as no commission will be forthcoming from the airline? TMCs argue that if they are not paid for selling, productivity will decrease. Other parties respond that you need to move from shifting costs to delivering value.

Companies want to know the total cost of a trip, which poses a challenge, as the fees are no longer just incurred upon booking, but at some point between the booking and the return of the traveler. In between a range of additional services are used, which can be assigned only with difficulty to the actual trip. Companies want transparency, control, reporting and reconciliation. The credit card companies are also working on solving this problem, so that all costs can be assigned to one and the same trip.

3.6 Social media and travel

At the beginning of 2010, Facebook had more than 500 million active users [83]. If Facebook were a country, it would be the third largest after China (1.34 billion) and India (1.2 billion) and ahead of the United States (308 million)[84]. One out of every 8 couples getting married met via social media[85]. A number of websites offer impressive statistics[86].

An affiliation is often initiated by "word-of-mouse" – the latest version of "word-of-mouth". There is also the concept known as "customer-to-customer marketplace" (C2C), analogous to B2C, B2E, etc., as products are sold by one customer to another via social media.

The concepts "next gen web" (next generation web) or Web 2.0 do not represent any fundamentally new technologies or applications; rather, these describe a sociotechnical change in the use of the Internet, in which its potentials are consistently utilized and further developed. Social software solutions such as Twitter, Facebook, etc. are not only tools with which to procure information; they change the process and the culture of how to deal with each other. They create added value, as one can participate in others' activities and can learn from them; they strengthen connections between friends as well as companies, and they generate transparency.

The usefulness of social media and Web 2.0 (or Web 3.0 in the next phase) might be discussed controversially. However there is no doubt that social media will have an impact on the travel industry. The fact is social media is ubiquitous and here to stay. As mentioned in the first paragraph, Facebook alone had already more active users in 2010 than the United States had inhabitants. Other internet giants, such as Google want to establish a competitive social media platform as well.

In 2000 advertising and marketing measures were still crucial to the success of touristic services. No one could check the quality in advance. Today it's completely different - nobody buys a "pig in a poke" any more. Customers can not only inform themselves about their destination via the Internet (thus preventing surprises such as hotels located next to the airport instead of at the beach), but virtually fly there using e.g. Google Maps and gain initial impressions via YouTube, Flickr, etc. With Web 2.0 this information is now supplemented by comments and feedback from other guests.[87] Customers thus become "communication media", the "voice" of a company, acting as advertisers (with positive feedback) and critics (negative feedback). Social media will therefore play a central role in marketing and its word of mouth/mouse campaign. Every company should know how it is represented in all media and take steps if necessary to promote positive aspects and cushion negative ones. Previously, travelers' criticisms were disseminated in their local pubs and neighborhoods - today, negative or sarcastic feedback reaches the entire virtual world.

If one extrapolates the trends of the social networks, they could be distribution channels within ten years. Travel providers will soon be trying to market their products via social networks. According to

Forrester, every second American flight passenger trusts content placed online by like-minded people - a lone top position. Only every third person trusts the supplier websites, and only every fifth person places any credence in television commercials.

The fundamental slogan for the social web is indeed "Conversations, Not Campaigns", which is the reason that defining metrics to measure success and Return On Investment (ROI) through traditional means is next to impossible, thus pointing out the primary problem with this communication channel. And yet it will not be long before remainders, at a minimum, or special offers are marketed via the various social platforms. For example, it would be easy to integrate an order form into a Facebook fan page using a specifically programmed application which facilitates accessing databases or back-ends to book services without leaving the website.

Over time, travelers will demand information faster and with less effort, which means that changes in the booking process will be necessary. In this context, consumers (not only in the travel industry) will demand more efficient access to relevant information than they now do, so that in the future all intermediate steps must be eliminated. Customers must be offered a point of sale without detours from whichever site they visit in their spare time - Facebook, Flickr, YouTube, Twitter, TripAdvisor, etc.

"Intelligent agent Web", "Web 3.0", "semantic Web", "data Web" or "bot Web" are all terms which mean that the familiar applications interact with each other without user intervention or knowledge. This is inconceivable in a protectionist world (think of Amadeus and Sabre exchanging all their data with each other), because neither would give the other party anything at all that might help it advance. In contrast, in the Internet mutual assistance is very common, e.g., in the open source initiative: somebody programs something and makes it available to the community. This idea is taken further and the applications help each other reciprocally to become even more intelligent. Although the Internet is a fantastic source of information, all that content was not in machine-readable format. Now, the variety and volume of information increased so much that a human alone can no longer process it. Thus intelligent machines, supported by minimal human supervision and proofreading are needed to process all that information and separate the wheat from the chaff.

Take TripIt, for example: TripIt gets its content from any number of sources (travelers themselves, rental car companies, airlines, consumers, travel agencies, restaurants, cruise lines, etc.) and distributes it in turn to social networks such as LinkedIn, mobile applications or internal corporate networks, all without the users noticing any of its activity.

From the standpoint of data protection, that sounds fairly dangerous, but it is a new trend that the industry needs to follow. Travelers need to understand this as well; the industry must do its part to explain this to them and point out the options available. This is yet another reason why the industry should not spend too much time navel-gazing, but needs to enter the 21st century at last, albeit a decade late. If the players in the travel industry do not get their act together, the users will do it for them: already today the typical business traveler has already become a rational end customer, as the TMCs will confirm. With more than 14,000 applications (See section 3.1) available on the market, the travelers know more about their trip than their agent. This is a factor to be taken seriously: why should you pay an agent who knows less than you do? On the other hand, no agent can learn the specific requirements of every single traveler. The only way for an agent to solve this conundrum is for a machine to do this work for him and provide the best information possible about the needs of the traveler in conjunction with the interests of the company. The technology must provide advice to the agent (and the agent to the customer), e.g., that a good alternative would be to book the hotel directly across from the meeting location even though it costs USD 50 more (and thus would violate the travel policies). Why? The daily costs of a rental car and parking or other transport would be eliminated.

The industry needs to use intelligent agents for its own purposes. In this context the term "intelligent agent[88]" is used for a computer and shall not be confused with "smart travel agents". Intelligent agents — can automatically and periodically seek out the best offers in accordance with the travelers' preferences without a human having to do two hours of research. They can provide support for quick decisions, e.g., like when a traveler is stuck in a traffic jam and may miss a flight. They are the key to having more time for yourself and your family in the future.

3.7 Door-to-door, Geo data and trip management

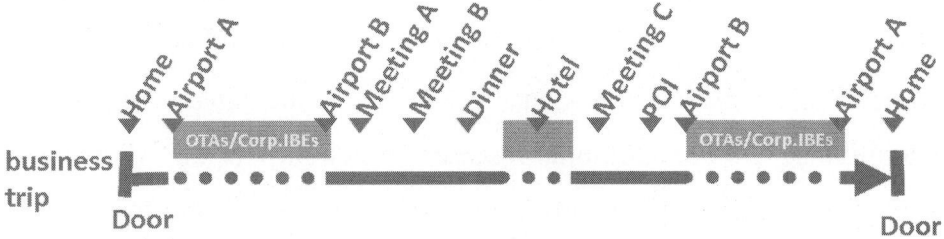

Figure 13: Door-to-door locations

A trip does not start at the airport and end there. It actually starts at your doorstep, leads to your final destination which might be a meeting at location A then B, a dinner, and a meeting at location C the next day. Travel Management today usually only covers flights and hotels along with rentals cars potentially with navigation systems, which does not mean that all destinations are optimized, that the hotel is booked between destination B and C, that the return airport is close to your location C while the destination airport is close to your first meeting (Meeting A). Current systems usually only cover the grey parts in the picture – everything in between has to be handled by the traveler himself or his agent. There is a huge potential in providing improved consultation/information to the traveler for the areas in between.

Geo data services not only offer travelers the option of searching for the best flight connections from nearby airports but also an optimized comparison of transportation means. Taxis, rental cars, public transportation and one's own vehicle are considered in order to determine the simplest, fastest or most affordable journey to the desired destination. Thus, for example, it might be faster or more cost-effective on particular days or at certain times to drive or take the train to a neighboring airport and fly directly to the desired destination instead of taking a connecting flight. Without Geo data service, business people from the US who want to visit e.g., SAP[89] would have a tough time determining, without additional research, which airport and what means of transportation are best to reach Walldorf. Moreover, the user is offered additional information on sightseeing or points of interest such as hotels, restaurants, movie theaters or gas stations along the route and near the destination. Thus the Geo data service is an efficient tool that gives the user an overview of all options available in just a few seconds. This saves business travelers a lot of time, because they no longer have to cobble together the required information from multiple websites. Moreover, queries can be optimized according to cost or time savings: Information on the destination area, suggestions, location-independent services and ideas top off the service. Trips are already booked through a great number of media in various systems. Recurring data (personal data, profiles, bookings, etc.) have to be entered and maintained redundantly. This calls for IT systems that handle the comparison of data while at the same time ensuring its confidentiality.

3.8 Further trends

A lot has happened in the travel industry in a very short time. Groundbreaking innovations were still rare in 2008, but in the meantime innumerable mobile applications and new ideas are everywhere. The shift toward new trends can no longer be halted and is growing exponentially at ever shorter intervals[90]. Here are just a few hints of what is happening:

- Virtualization: Years ago the matrix display was a groundbreaking thing. Today, it's the linking of the ticket and price. (Where can one fly for USD 700? Where's my plane?, etc.) HTML 5.0, expanded video capabilities, scalable vector graphics, Geo data and WebTV will bring a flood of visual applications.
- Crisis management: Swine flu, SARS, oil disaster, terror attacks, catastrophes, earthquakes, political unrest such as turmoil, riot, war, etc. are sources of concern in our times. Handling crises is part of professional travel management today. "Where are my travelers? How do I get them out of the danger zone? What do's and don'ts should I give them?" Advising the traveler does not stop once the booking is done; it continues throughout the journey until the guest is at home again, safe and sound.
- Voice recognition: The days of the computerized voice which simply cannot understand the caller are over. Voice recognition systems are viable only for particular services, must be capable of short, concise dialogs and inspire positive feedback from the caller with their efficiency. That means quick, competent processing of the call. In the travel sector that means that the booking should be found and made available automatically for incoming calls based on the caller's number. The situation must anticipate the traveler's thoughts or concerns using typical behavior patterns. "Mr. Miller, I see that you are booked on Lufthansa flight 463 to Miami. The plane will depart on time in exactly two hours. Since you are on your way to the airport at the

moment, would you like to check in now?" The system must provide more than relief for the call center; more importantly it should enhance the traveler's experience. In no way should the system irritate the traveler with questions that the system should already know the answer to, such as "Which flight are you on?", "Where do you depart from?", etc.

- Price forecasts, auctions, price alarms, automatic bookings and even augmented reality are trends which will have a significant influence on travel. Machines will communicate with each other, enhancing one another so that a better option can be found. Travelers will take pictures or videos, objects will be recognized and background information will be provided. In short, there will no longer be a shortage of information, but rather a challenge to process the amount of information and make use of it wisely. This is one of the greatest challenges for IT in the near future.

- RFID will become widespread available. Eventually it will also enter the travel industry and make tasks such as boarding easier. Recently Apple applied for a patent in regards to its iTravel application[91] which incorporates such a means of checking-in and boarding.

- In early 2010, Google announced that it was in the market for partners in the travel industry (compare Section 5). Soon after Google acquired ITA software for a reported USD 700 million (baring regulatory approval). Forrester Research explained that Google's mission is to organize the world's information, and that is what ITA does for travel. Forrester was not surprised that

Google was showing interest; they are just surprised that it took them this long to start acting. PhoCusWright's Consumer Travel Report Second Edition shows that Google might actually need this enhancement to stay relevant to travelers: Consumers who usually or exclusively book online are significantly less likely to use search engines while shopping for travel – they go straight to the brands they already know. Similar deals for the hotel and rental car segment remain to be seen.

4 Future scenario 1: evolution

4.1 Suppliers

Suppliers – foremost among them the airlines – want to continue to expand direct sales and also build their presence in the business segment. Today they already dominate online sales. (Seventy percent of online sales are through supplier websites, 30% via OTAs.) Furthermore, they will attempt to make themselves independent of the GDSs by no longer managing their inventory in a GDS. Merchandising (See section 3.5) or 'unbundling' of fares is another major trend with some airlines, particularly in the US. The price of the ticket may possibly play only a minor role. However, the problem for the airlines remains that they all sell the same product: a seat. Airlines must differentiate themselves and instead sell experiences and emotions. In the future, moreover, providers will make their content available through each channel on different terms. For example, airlines might contract directly with sales channels, such as travel agencies, portals or TMCs. Thus they could 'compel' distribution for better utilization. Increasing numbers of passengers might board a plane and book the rest of the trip (i.e., hotel and rental car) there; hotels and rental car agencies would have to be prepared to take bookings on the go. There will probably also be last-minute marketplaces and location dependent services that will focus on offering unused inventory or fare allotments to customers passing by/through.

In the course of airlines reinventing themselves, distribution costs also came to light. During the time when several airlines were faced with insolvency proceedings they refrained from taking actions against their distribution partner (Distributors can, after all, control the business in such a way that an airline is driven to ruin). Distribution costs however (particularly commissions for a sale) have always been a source of irritation for airlines. With the rise of low cost carriers, which in some cases were not in the GDSs but enjoyed a booming business using the Internet, there was a new model to imitate. Today every airline is well represented on the Internet. As the figures show in section 1.4, half of the leisure travelers book directly over the supplier's website. Business trips are the next segment to be addressed, not only to reduce those margins for distributors as well, but primarily because the use of new technologies enables airlines to collect additional fees (merchandising – see Section 3.4). GDSs also joined the march toward ancillary revenue after some delay, but it is questionable whether the airlines will allow them a share of the take. Their tardiness in bringing necessary technologies to the market in a timely manner will cost GDSs dearly. Airlines have found their own footing and if necessary will sell directly to companies with the help of new technologies made manageable and robust by startups. As always, if there is a niche, there will always be companies ready to fill it enthusiastically.

The travel organizer market is focused on providing a simple offer which is easy to understand and is matched to the traveler's needs. Organizers can profit from the fact that two-thirds of travelers are dissatisfied with their respective online experiences and just under a fourth would prefer a good offline agency.

The tour operator market, which is predominant in Europe, also shows some technology challenges: most organizers are currently focused on developing a new core system which enables dynamic pricing and packaging.[92] A dangerous side effect is that procurement[93] is no longer restricted to an exclusive group of partners and the market is thus becoming more transparent. The quantities of data pose an enormous technological challenge. While in the past there were 1500 records to process, today with all the possible combinations the number approaches 15 million. These can no longer be handled effectively with the prevailing INFX[94] interface. Structures must be broken up, and an open standard for tourism must be created.

4.2 Distribution

GDSs understand how to jump on the bandwagon of new trends and secure a good future for themselves with various sources of business. Thus all GDSs have already founded OTAs and operate them successfully. At the same time they are also establishing OTMCs and ITMCs on the market. So GDSs are not as old-fashioned as they are usually perceived (as legacy systems more or less). Of course they attempt nonetheless to defend their traditional business and keep newcomers out as much as possible. This will remain the case until they are required by law or forced by the market to allow fair competition. (See also Section 2.4, the box on protectionism)

Global distribution systems have also positioned themselves well with respect to their suppliers. Since in most cases they are still the reservation system for the airlines, they claim ownership of the PNR and all those wanting access must make arrangements with them. The same applies to the traveler's profile.

The GDSs control the inventory of providers, make their technology available to both the providers and sellers, handle distribution globally and have a significant influence on the distribution of commissions. They are nearly impossible to bypass. This is quite a victory when one considers their origins as simple technology supplier. Who can deny that technology is the key? And the best part is that all this is accomplished with a manageable financial investment: a few data centers, some offices and developers, but no Boeing or Airbus craft, no 2700 ft high hotels, mega-cruise liners or a rental car fleet. And in cases of doubt GDSs have enough cash on hand to quash aspiring newcomers or acquire them and maintain control this way.

There is a danger that those who do not stand on their own and who have put all their eggs in the GDS basket will lose out, i.e., agencies and TMCs. In addition GDSs control inventory, technology, distribution and commission.

The danger to the future of GDSs is from direct distribution. Here a race against time prevails among competitors. It can indeed be more lucrative for an airline to distribute via less expensive channels (See section 3.2,

2.2). However, the example of Lufthansa's preferred fares shows that GDSs with their cash power are well positioned to work against this. Thus in 2009 Amadeus paid the fee demanded by Lufthansa so that no agents migrated from the Amadeus platform to another one. Consequently their control of the agencies and thus their core business remained intact. The question usually becomes: who will run out of money first in this dispute: investors in the direct connection platform or GDSs?

General consensus in the industry is that GDSs need to transform into global merchandising (see Section 3.4) systems. GDSs today already rely on a multi-GDS strategy, because it is obvious that not one of them can rule the world alone. They open up among themselves, but they are not yet to the point of generally opening up to everyone. This step is inevitable. A system is only as good as the weakest link in the chain and not even all three global distribution systems together can claim to have all content. That means they must open up to a multi-source strategy. The question is only when they will recognize this and whether someone else will fill the niche first, or whether it will be mandated by law.

There could also be further consolidations, because there are IPOs time and again and the financial markets ask hard questions. Since contracts with the airlines usually run for five years, there is a risk of an avalanche effect: an airline could choose another provider and others follow. Therefore along with rumors of GDS mergers among themselves there are rumors of merger with a TMC in order to control the entire distribution and sales process.

4.3 Sales

Two thirds of all trips were already being booked online in 2009. Two thirds of those online bookers shopped with OTAs, while 70% booked directly from the supplier. This does not call for a high closing rate. Studies[95] show the clear dissatisfaction of those online shoppers: Two thirds of customers in 2009 complained that the online offerings were not clear and comprehensive. Twenty-three percent would even prefer a traditional travel agency over online research. However, this is not that the traditional agencies simplify the booking process, but rather that the OTAs present the selections badly and that the volume of information to be processed by the person booking is unreasonable. Thus conventional travel agencies have a good chance of a renaissance and ought to use it. A professional website is part of this exercise, of course. Customers want to gather information themselves, want to be inspired online, while the agent in turn can provide more specific advice if the person being helped has already gathered some basic knowledge online. The traditional travel agency of the future will be virtualized and develop into a "virtual adventure park". Before the customer has booked his vacation he will have already received firsthand impressions and experienced a taste of the destination area in the travel agency. No more expensive catalogs: the customer will put together a trip himself with the touch screen function on a large display. The agent will become an entertainer.

HOW TRADITIONAL AGENCIES CAN COME OUT AHEAD:

1. Specialize in topics such as scuba diving, skiing, golf and offer their products and services interregionally
2. Be represented offline as well as online
3. Have a good technology platform and consequently be able to market the best products and services at fair prices
4. Be able to advise the customer and demonstrate superior product knowledge
5. Save the customer research time with the best offer. This does not have to be the lowest price, but rather a fair offer in a reasonable timeframe at a fair price with minimal risk.
6. Provide information on the destination area and Geo data as well as information on protection and safety.
7. Grow into the role of a "travel designer" and "lifestyle consultant" for leisure travelers or "travel time optimizer" and "stress reducer" in the business world and thus build a bridge between desire and reality for the customer.

Travel agencies must become travel consultants.

The added value of an agent in the future should no longer lie in fast system operation – IT must provide this – but rather in offering the best advice to customers. So they must have flawless knowledge of the destination region and be able to foster the interests of the traveler. This would lead to specialization among the travel agencies. The limiting factor for a travel agency is not so much the local border to the next town but rather the professional know-how and knowledge of the destination within the agency.

In the business travel segment TMCs and GDSs appear to get along quite well; not surprising, since the GDSs pay the commissions. But appearances are deceptive: GDSs give most TMCs their desktop solutions and thus ensure a special kind of customer loyalty from the TMC. In this case the GDSs control the heartbeat of the TMC: the system with which the agents work. At the same time GDSs also operate competing systems. TMCs must take care not to become the losers in the battle between airlines and GDSs.

Are the TMCs ready for a change? Are they able to stand on their own? There is really no "good" time for a change. A slump in travel volume due to the financial crisis, high fuel prices, service fees, the sale of special services and merchandising, shareholder value, acquisitions in new markets, you name it: Change means moving out of one's comfort zone. No one likes doing that. But sometimes it's a good idea to reshape the future in advance of the last possible moment before an impending disaster. Moreover, consider the age of the agents: as previously mentioned, according to a study in the US, 80 % of them are over 45 and most still work with the cryptic command-based systems of the old days.

TMCs must learn to move with the trends instead of remaining entrenched in the status quo. The travel industry suggests that distribution costs are too high. At the same time direct distribution suggests that the sales chain is too long. History shows that it is generally not the company with the greatest financial strength which survives, but rather the one with the right strategy and the right technology. Those companies which continually reinvent themselves and make radical changes at the right time usually thrive. This is a wake-up call for TMCs! How well are they positioned?

WHAT DOES A TMC ACTUALLY DO?

From a corporate perspective, the basic functions of a TMC include:

1. Booking, changing or canceling trips, including ensuring compliance with corporate policies and the use of preferred rates;

2. Provision of a call center for complex trips as well as an online booking tool for simple trips (and support for it – however, keep in mind that they generally have no online booking tool of their own);

3. Have representation (internationally) in the location that the business for which travel is managed has a subsidiary, an important customer, a supplier, or a significant volume of travel for some other reason;

4. Support through consulting and global reports, assurances that commitments will be kept, that the level of services steadily increase while costs are reduced, that redundancies will be avoided and that future contract negotiations aim for these objectives;

5. Delivering content and inventory from sources which offer the best value for the company.

The services also include a 24/7 helpdesk, catastrophe management (location and support of traveling employees), the planning of meetings and incentive programs.

The competition soon felt by the TMCs from the GDSs is something leisure agents supposedly know well: Leisure agencies have already ceded two thirds of the market to the OTAs, which are mostly operated by GDSs. These in turn have lost business to the suppliers. Today OTAs book about 10 to 15 % of the overall travel revenues in developed countries.

However, the current OTA market also reveals a system gone awry: travelers use OTAs to shop but then book directly on the supplier websites. Altogether just three out of ten online users book online through an OTA, while two out of three do their research with OTAs. In other words, the OTAs fail to close the deal half the time. Conversely, suppliers in fact profit from the OTAs: Although only 40 % of the online users use the suppliers' websites to search, 70 % of all online deals are closed there. Even the elimination of the mandatory booking fee by the OTAs was not able to slow this trend. Moreover, this measure is the subject of dispute; according to PhoCusWright, OTAs must increase their bookings by 45 to 90 %[96] to compensate fully for the cost of this measure. The OTA share of flight bookings would then have to increase from 32 % to between 46-61 %. Thus it is no wonder that 2009 saw the first decline in booking figures for OTAs. In their heyday in 2002, OTAs enjoyed more than 50 % of online bookings. On the other hand, recognizing the trends and viewing the matter from the perspective of innovation, there are still many opportunities here. Products and services for travel are increasing in complexity (see, for example, Section 3.2, 3.5 and 3.2), and the customer can be spared much stress and effort if all aspects of a trip booking (air travel, car, hotel, etc.) are handled by a single provider as long as that provider can be trusted to take the traveler's personal needs into account. Information technology can provide support for this.

IS THE OTA OBSOLETE?

The competition on the market is tough and well entrenched among discounters. Specialization and simplification are the keys here. Users will no longer tolerate having to penetrate 200 unfiltered combinations with transfers. The information displayed must be clear and simple. Information with added value must be included. The trip must begin at the traveler's doorstep and lead to the destination (including geographic information), not just from airport to airport. Intelligence and user preferences must be integrated at the search stage. For a flight from A to B and back to A with the same airline, the customer has no disadvantage booking directly with the supplier. OTAs could experience a renaissance if

- An OTA provides the technical option to show the best connection – in other words, to include planning for the customer's actual starting point (not just the airport), with regard to the latest departure flight and the most sensible return time and/or fare and/or route optimized according to personal preferences, regardless of airline.

- At the same time it should be ensured that the customer is just as well positioned as if the booking had been made directly with the airline (for example, guaranteed seat reservation, the OTA takes care of changes and does not leave the customer on his own to call the airline, etc.).

- For combined bookings (i.e., air, hotel and rental car), one step shopping/booking should provide a clear time-saving benefit.

- This means, however, that the OTAs must get away from shopping functions which are optimized for the price alone and are throughout the industry provided by the same technology providers (i.e., ITA software or GDSs).

- There are fares which are not in the GDS or the respective website of the supplier (consolidator fares). These fares even with a margin for the OTA might still offer a bargain and must be further exploited.

- Along with the price, the qualitative objectives must influence the search results. Search criteria must be individually adaptable. Geo data, mobile and social media will soon be standard.

Given the pace of the internet age, in a few years, perhaps even months, additional trends could develop which require a response. This means that the main platform must be flexible enough to integrate these trends, even the ones that no one can imagine today. If this is not taken into account, OTAs could quickly find themselves again in the situation that requires their IT system to be completely rewritten every two years or else they will disappear from the market.

Meta search engines provide an alternative to the desired one stop shop: Meta search engines screen scrape supplier websites as well as OTAs and other sources and provide such an offer in a well-designed flexible and customizable form to the client. They started a couple of years later than OTAs and thus utilize newer, more flexible technology. Since meta search engines do not provide booking capabilities themselves, their business model consists of receiving a referral fee from the source from which a trip is finally booked. Currently OTAs as well as suppliers happily pay this fee in the area of USD 5 per booking as these are very valuable "leads" of prospects who have finished shopping and will soon make a purchasing decision. As the usual cost for the acquisition of one traveler is in the area close to USD 20, the fee to meta search engines seems like a bargain. Since these "leads" however will most likely continue to use meta search engines for their shopping, it remains in doubt whether such a lead can be converted or if one continues to pay for the same lead over and over. Today however meta search engines are sometimes biased and prefer providing fares that pay for placement. It also remains to be seen how general search engine providers such as Google will enter this space and when (especially with the help of their newly acquired shopping engine from ITA software[97]). According to PhoCusWright, meta search companies are now required to build true consumer brands – something beyond a collection of features, functions, widgets and gadgets to survive the upcoming era of disruption. And they had better do it fast. A combination of meta search functionality, consolidator fares, fulfillment capabilities, and an online/mobile presence together with a highly qualified offline call center might be a well-positioned sales entity for the future.

4.4 End users and businesses

For years, companies have tried to use the same TMC for all their locations worldwide. At the same time, the TMC claims that there is no single online booking tool that works the best in all regions. There is also no GDS that is preferred in all regions. Thus today, travel managers for a multi-regional company select their online booking tool according to region, the GDS according to region, preferred airlines according to region, preferred hotel chains according to region and yet a single TMC for all over the world.

But why should not every employee work with the same booking interface and the technology work out the differences (back-office, statutory requirements, etc.)? Why should one not select the best local agency even if it not part of a huge chain? The art of being the company travel manager is to handle these conflicts of interest. Business models, too, do not fit every company. Take the transaction-dependent pricing of solutions, for example: An online solution for a company must work as well for 100 employees as it does for 100,000. Why should one company pay five million dollars for this while another invests only USD 5000 during the year based on transactions?

The creativity of employees must also not be underestimated. Today's tools must support or facilitate flexibility so that humans are not made servants of the machine. There are companies in which every employee is at liberty to make bookings themselves wherever they choose up to a maximum amount. About half of the travel volume in those companies is booked[98] following business policies on the free market by employees - in some cases with greater success than with the use of tools. Employees thus not only have the opportunity to save the company money; they also have the chance to consider their private interests. For example, an employee stayed in Santa Monica, California for a mere

USD 42 per night where hotels are seldom found for under USD 200 per night. When asked about this, it was revealed that he had rented a camper on the beach and went surfing every morning before work.

4.5 Technology and target architecture

The four most important requirements for technology are:

1. Flexibility: Above all, the application must be flexible and allow a certain amount of adaptability without involving the developer.
2. Ease of use: The user interface must be intuitive with a high level of recognizability. Different sources of content must have the same interface. Recurring functions must be automated. The user interface must learn.
3. Maintainability: The technology should be based on reusable modules and follow the SOA approach. Each service must be built as such and be addressable by other modules. Services must be able to be integrated internally and externally. Ultimately, new business processes should be defined by a business analyst and saved in the technology without involving a programmer.
4. Configurability/Scalability: In the future, certain business processes will be able to change minute by minute. Maintainability and flexibility already cover quite a lot, but it will still be necessary to change individual actions "on the fly".

All this goes hand in hand, of course. For the basic system, one must consider whether things are handled by configuration, rules or maintenance.

WHAT SERVICES MUST TECHNOLOGY OFFER TODAY?

The requirements are broad, but some common points can be identified:
- Independent testing:
    - Functionality and user interface, including n-tier architecture in .NET and J2EE
    - Compatibility with browsers and application servers with multiple operating systems, social media and mobile applications (Section 3.1)
    - Security (authentication, SQL & HTML injections, cross-site scripting, cookie recycling & SSL usage)
    - SOAP, XML, WSDL, Web services interoperability
    - Performance, load and scalability, localization and globalization
- Integration of services:
    - Integration with Geo data, local city guides, weather forecasts (Section 3.7), social networking sites (Section 3.6), etc.
    - Integration with payment systems
    - Integration with third-party providers (GDS, online hotel or rental car service providers, recommendation providers, UGC, other websites, etc.)
    - Purchasing decisions based on "good enough" vs. "best of breed"
- Integration of current consumer requirements:
    - Software as a service / cloud applications
    - Cloud services, social computing that includes blogs, etc.
    - Open-source software
    - Real-time (such as Google Wave, chatting with friends or

- customers)
- Universal access
- Web communication
- Decentralized systems
- Modular / reusable design
- Heavily networked
- Video
- New user interfaces
- Social customer service
- Ranking
- Virtual conferencing (Section 3.3)
- Voice control (Section 3.8)
- Architecture:
  - Service-oriented architecture (SOA)
  - Event-based architecture
  - Unified access to content and data
  - Build: mash-up, process modeling, business rules
  - Outsourcing options with top performance and the highest level of security, but without expensive certifications (PCI[99] compliance, etc.)

In Section 2.4 it was described that the cannibalistic nature of the market allows for no definitive, long-term strategy, because new challenges are faced continually. For example, if a supplier of technology needs an agent desktop application today, tomorrow it might be a corporate booking IBE. One thing that is clear is that whatever effort is made, it should not be wasted. Everything must be reusable. Today most tools have their own logic; tomorrow they must be networked. No consumer wants to have to make changes to numerous websites including social media, bank- shopping- and travel accounts because of a change of address or workplace. Nevertheless, today traveler profiles are managed in the GDS, at the TMC, the leisure agency, various supplier sites, customer loyalty measures, CRMs, OTAs, OTMCs, etc.: a real nightmare. The systems must work together. Each should do what it does best. The computers must communicate with each other in the background (see also Section 3.6). Nonetheless, security and privacy must be ensured. This is no easy task, but that is not an excuse for inaction. Rules and process engines used which, as in Section 4.5, must be completely flexible, since no business will want to create and maintain rules for each desktop solution, corporate booking tool, mobile API and voice interface separately.

Yet that is exactly the situation today. Currently the industry makes itself slaves to technology instead of making technology serve its purposes. Has all travel prosperity and technology led to more time with families and less at work? No. Though the physical labors are no longer as hard as they were a century ago, office hours have not changed. For example, travelers must structure their processes in the company according to what is possible with the off-the-shelf corporate booking tool, exactly as determined by the producer of the tool. This is the situation, despite the fact that the travel volume of an investment firm, an oil company, a manufacturer or a consulting firm differ fundamentally. However, if one switches the vertical and horizontal axes, things might look much better: an individual process logic and rules engine for the individual company with all its specific worldwide requirements and all booking interfaces are built on this.

How might such an architecture look? It could be a sandwich consisting of a process engine (workflow engine) and a transaction server which controls and secures the connections to third-party systems.

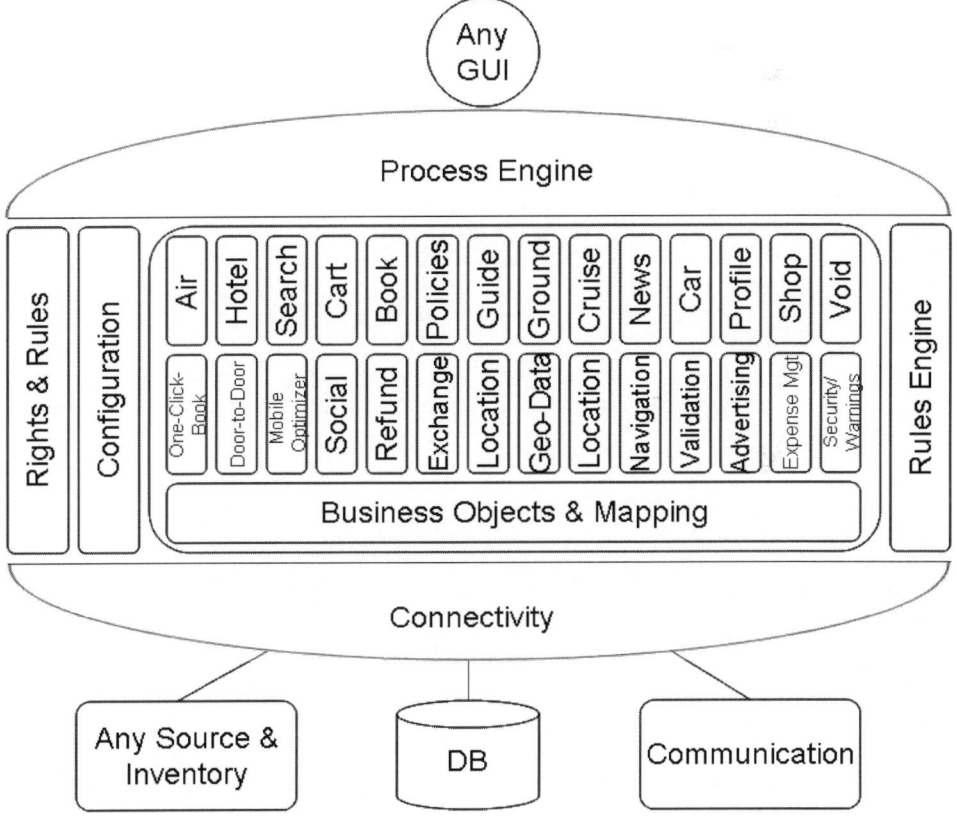

Figure 14: Flexible travel distribution technology architecture

Its core consists of internal and external services and business objects, which together with the rights and roles component, the configuration tool and the rules engine constitutes the business logic. Like an olive, the "sandwich" is embellished with a graphical user interface which is adapted to the particular characteristics of the area in which it is used (mobile, desktop, call center, etc.). There will be no "one size fits all" product to meet modern requirements for travel and business trips in particular. Individual travel solutions that fulfill all wishes must be based on the principle that, on one hand, the business shapes the technology and, on the other hand, the design of individual processes must encounter no limitations.

5 Future scenario 2: Revolution

A revolution means that the leap is made directly to the next generation. Progress or a fundamental change does not take place slowly and gradually, but quickly and in grand style. An entire unit is transformed in a short period of time. Intermediate steps are omitted. In contrast to this, evolution occurs in incremental steps over a longer period of time.

In the travel industry a revolution could take place with an operator from outside the sector who has the necessary funds and infrastructure, entering the industry and exercising significant influence on the market. That could happen if someone with the necessary means and market leverage recognizes the importance of travel distribution itself and wants to capitalize on it.

5.1 Revolution initiated by an industry expert

Here one might think first of a technology provider who already has its foot in the travel industry's door, who analyzes the market, identifies weak points, organizes a new order and thus expands its footprint. IBM or HP would certainly be in a position to start a revolution. Take, for example, HP/EDS, which will host the inventory of American Airlines (AA) in the future – a task assumed from Sabre (See section 4.2). This amounts to the GDS losing control over the inventory. Furthermore, since AA uses its own sales channel and offers merchandising (See section 3.5) via this channel only, GDSs are also compelled to handle this interface. Let's assume, moreover, that AA succeeds in persuading

TMCs and leisure agents to use an alternative distribution channel, one for which they need only a front end to work efficiently. This would set the stage. So far the GDSs have avoided this scenario successfully, because their inventory may not be shown on the same screen with other inventory. The GDSs also continue to attempt to retain their tools as the front end of the agencies and TMCs and thus GDSs can exercise control over their agents. But assume that TMCs get away from this and use their own front end that they either develop themselves or have developed by technology firms. Then they would be independent and in control of distribution.

Now one could go a step farther and leave out the TMCs. In other words, businesses use their own corporate IBE with in-house agents operating their own multi-function desktop. In that case, distribution in 2020 might well take place without TMCs and GDSs. This scenario would significantly simplify distribution and enable it to be controlled more cost-effectively and strictly by the parties concerned. Technology is the enabler of revolution. Fragmentation might still be caused by political barriers, but should not be put in place by technology.

What does the situation with expense management and the back office look like? Here, too, there could be a big bang. Currently, all expenses are consolidated via the GDS. They might be compared with credit card data as required. If merchandising (See section 3.5) however can no longer be completely documented via the GDS, the "whole truth" about a business trip lies in the corporate credit card data. This also includes expenses for fuel, meals, invitations, etc. With a connection (or feeds) from the credit card company any software firm can be hired to report and evaluate this data and thus enable the business to manage and optimize their travel expenses.

In the past, GDSs were 'misused' as databases and have built their business model on this fact. Back when GDSs were established databases such as Oracle, etc., they were expensive. However today it is a different ball game. Thus what would happen if 'real' databases were used for data storage in the travel market? Performance has to be evaluated for sure. Other than this, the only thing putting players off from this is the complicated migration associated with a change in the core infrastructure. "Never touch a running system" is the old saying, but at some point things no longer work and migration becomes necessary.

5.2 Revolution initiated by a newcomer outside the sector

A newcomer to the sector could also enter just as well as a strong player close to the industry. Examples of candidates here are the three Internet giants: Google, Microsoft and Apple along with a wild card such as Facebook. Apple shocked the travel industry in mid-2010 with its patent for iTravel, which not only speeds up the check-in process using RFID but also maps the entire travel process.

After these announcements there was great fear that Apple would not merely enter the travel industry but would even take it over – as they did with the music industry (over 25% of songs are sold via iTunes in the US[100]).

Apple revolutionized the music industry because the industry itself did not want to move into a new era and tried to preserve the status quo[101] while complaining about illegal Internet downloads.

Instead of adapting to a new age and being innovative and creative with the new tools provided by the Internet, the music industry chose to fight popular music sharing sites such as Napster[102], unknowingly creating a lack of innovation. The demand for new methods of distribution was present, but the music industry wanted to "preserve the old ways".

The telecommunication industry underwent a similar experience. Since 1998, traditional phone manufacturers had failed to make money with mobile data beyond the Short Message Service (SMS). They tried to force their clients to adapt to a limited keyboard and a small screen. Cell phones progressed from bulky to flat, from long to flip phones and from black/white to color displays, while the price always remained the focus of attention. It was expected that people would not pay for a high quality device, even though it was the one device which they carried with them at all times.

Then along came Apple and changed two simple rules: combine keyboard and screen to create a larger screen and a full keyboard, and have the customer pay a premium for a high-quality designer phone.

Thus a "nobody" entered the market and carried off significant revenues. In fact, while the stock price of the largest phone manufacturer worldwide crashed from USD 40 to USD 7 (Nokia)[103], Apple's increased from USD 120 to USD 260[104]. Nokia still has almost 40% of the market worldwide and Apple is not even among the top five, but almost certainly Apple caused some serious headaches at headquarters in Finland.

The level of innovation in the travel industry is not the highest and major players decided to negotiate instead of innovate. The industry itself created a gap which might be filled by players outside of the community because the travel industry as a group did not have the courage to work together for a better user experience. The industry has been resting on its laurels.

It's not just Apple: Microsoft[105] already runs its own travel service, and Google[106] (baring regulatory approval) acquired the dominant travel shopping engine (ITA software) causing a fundamental fear especially in the leisure sector since comprehensive price aggregation across sites is inevitable. Consumers will automatically receive real time fare results without necessarily doing anything different from what they do today. Eventually it might become a battle between the three Internet giants, while the traditional players in the travel industry will be fighting for the Oscar for the best supporting role.

Passengers might decide to store their profile and preferences in one trusted place, which might be Google. For Google and similar providers, it is a piece of cake to create or acquire a service such as TripIt, which enables travelers to forward their itineraries and store them in one place no matter where they were booked. This means travelers take control of their own travel needs, book directly and store everything in one place and thus eliminate the need for distribution at all. This is a nightmare scenario for businesses and their TMCs since they lose control of their employees. If employees share their trips freely on social media (Section 3.6) this might cause scenarios of espionage as competitors can simply find out who is meeting with whom. Similar to insurance companies which may soon charge a premium for Facebook and Twitter users since a large online audience can easily determine a convenient time to rob somebody's house, businesses need to establish a social media strategy to avoid having their competition find out about intended mergers or other means.

5.3 Revolution initiated by a newcomer outside the region:

An alternative scenario is that instead of an established western technology firm, a company from another country will take on the innovation gap and close it. Consider emerging countries like China and India, which will overtake western countries for travel in the medium term based on their domestic travel alone. If China, with its 1.3 billion citizens, and India, the world's largest democracy with 1.2 billion inhabitants, catch up to western standards, the travel volumes of the US with its 300 million people or Germany with 80 million will pale in comparison. Their advantage is that they start with state-of-the-art technology. The expectation is that the technology used, which will handle many times our travel volume and be based on the latest standards, will overtake our technologies, even if agents have moved beyond the cryptic commands of today's systems[107]. Commercial manufacturing is already established in China. Today, many products are no longer marked "Made in the USA" or "Made in Germany" but rather "Made in China". Cell-phone network technology, once the flagship of western nations, is no longer in its heyday, and even the largest network operator worldwide (Vodafone) uses technology from China today[108]. Car manufactures fear that they will lose ground in developing electric cars since China's battery technology is well advanced[109]. If the travel industry does not watch out and continues to undermine one another instead of working constructively together, Asia may soon dictate travel technology as well.

6 Future scenario 3: revolution with evolution

The best experiences show that revolutionary goals ought to be achieved with evolutionary means. How then might all players work together successfully and create added value for the traveler?

GDSs must reinvent themselves and return to their actual role as providers of technology or databases. A separation of the global distribution systems into technology providers for front-end, intermediate and back-end systems and CRS as an open system accessible to all would make sense.

The cost of CRS systems should be settled according to quality. None should be denied access to content. Each provider would have to offer open interfaces which are fairly priced depending on the quality and performance demanded by the user: "all you can eat" or per transaction pricing. Ultimate control of what enters the CRSs should be in the hands of the airlines. The entire incentive model should be eliminated. Each player in the value creation chain must earn its keep and find someone who recognizes the added value and pays for it. Already today the traveler or business pays the whole bill: customers pay a price to the airline, which in turn pays an amount to the GDSs, which then sell incentives to the agencies. Are travelers interested in this model, and do they approve of their money being distributed this way? Is the company which pays for a trip and pays for a TMC satisfied that the TMC profits in two ways? Let the customer decide what and who he is willing to pay for services rendered.

A model which separates the interests of the GDS (distribution) and CRS (data storage) focuses each party on its core business and the unique selling point of the one is not expanded to impinge on the business model of the other.

The next area to consider would be distribution or the marketplace: here, too, the principle that "quality has its price" should apply, but not in a restrictive manner. Complicated systems which check more variations in less time have a higher price to cover their greater intelligence or their use of equipment such as hardware for shopping queries. But in principle it is simply passing on queries with a number of optimization rules which optimize not only according to price but also service and preferences. This would be an enormous network of diverse sources which must all communicate with each other for an immense volume of content: shopping and booking, routing, social, mobile, destination, etc. – some of this information cannot be imagined today and can only be processed by a computer. It is not known which services will be used in years to come as they may not be invented yet.

The agency or TMC must establish a personal relationship with each traveler – and the price must reflect this as well. There is the clientele which cares only about the lowest price. There is another which always insists on the best. Between these extremes are a thousand further differentiations. And agencies can specialize here as well. There should be full service as well as pay-per-use service.

A better future for travelers, in which they are once again the focal point of consideration, will come to pass through the effective use of technology and the integration of key trends in both the business models and the IT environment of those involved in the industry.

7 Glossary

Car Rental Management System: a computer reservation system for automobile and limousine rental

Central Reservation System: usually provided by the GDSs

corporate social responsibility: (CSR): a concept that serves as a basis for a company to integrate social and environmental issues in their corporate activities and in the interaction with stakeholders on a voluntary basis. Definition of the European Commission, Green Paper

Customer Relationship Management: (CRM) is a broadly recognized, widely-implemented strategy for managing and nurturing a company's interactions with customers, clients and sales prospects

GDS: A GDS aggregates and manages booking records, also known as Passenger Name Records (PNRs), which it has received from the individual suppliers. Thus a GDS is made up of the CRS network and forms the basis of offer referral

INFX format: a text file based on the standardized INFX interface in which the trips are made available according to date, room type, board and occupancy with sale prices. Each record is checked beforehand for allotment availability so that only dates which can be booked are read

Intelligent agents: In artificial intelligence, an intelligent agent (IA) is an autonomous entity which observes and acts upon an environment (i.e. it is an agent) and directs its activity towards achieving goals. In the travel industry it can be computers which act like a human being and repeat searches and workflows efficiently and error free

Interlining: (also known as "interline ticketing") is a voluntary commercial agreement between individual airlines to handle passengers traveling on itineraries that require multiple airlines

Meta search engine: A meta search engine is a search tool that sends user requests to several other search engines and/or databases and aggregates the results into a single list or displays them according to their source

Moore's Law: states that the complexity of integrated circuits doubles about every two years with minimal component costs. Complexity was understood by Gordon Moore, who formulated the principle in 1965, to be the number of circuit components on a computer chip. Originally Moore spoke of a doubling each year, but in 1975 he corrected his statement to every two years (see also Wirth's Law)

Online TMC or ITMC: (Internet TMC) – an online agency for the business travel market

Online travel agency: an agency with a predominantly online presence and minimal call center activity

Parent carriers are airlines which directly or indirectly, alone or in concert with other airlines or rail companies, own or effectively control system providers

PAX: is used when referring to the traveler in the airline industry

PNR: A PNR (Passenger Name Record) is an electronic record of all data and procedures related to a flight booking (or a hotel or rental car booking); the information is stored in the respective CRS for a particular period even after the flight

preferred fares: Fares which are made available to a select group of users via a GDS – so-called "preferred private fares". The price level of preferred fares is below that generally accessible via a GDS

Property Management System: the hotel's computer reservation system

SAP: is a company headquartered in Germany

screen scraping: Screen scraping is part of data scraping which is a technique in which a computer program extracts data from human-readable output coming from another program. Originally, screen scraping referred to the practice of reading text data from a computer terminal's screen. Modern screen scraping techniques in the case of GUI applications include querying the graphical controls by programmatically obtaining references to their underlying programming objects

SuperPNR: Using a super-PNR enables a travel management company to create its own record for each traveler's ticket, including name and contact information, separate from individual coding interfaces, freeing the TMC from relying on one GDS for full access to airline content
Source: http://www.businesstravelnews.com/More-News/Articles/BCD,-HRG-To-Deploy-Super-PNR-Systems/

Travel Management Company (TMC): a travel agency for the business travel market consisting of a call center and online sales

yield management: Yield management, also known as revenue management (RM), is the process of understanding, anticipating and influencing consumer behavior in order to maximize revenue or profits from a fixed, perishable resource (such as airline seats or hotel room reservations). Yield management is basically profit management, an instrument for simultaneous, dynamic, usually computerized control of prices and capacity. In the beginning it was used by airlines, hotels and car rental agencies; in the meantime other sectors such as theater, cinema, concerts and many others apply it

8 Footnotes

1. Central Reservation System – usually provided by the GDSs

2. Companies which aggregate (combine) services offered by various sources

3. Consolidators have contracts, for example with airlines, for acquiring large quantities of seating capacity. As large volume purchasers they receive a discount, which is passed on to customers with a margin surcharge

4. Travel Management Company (TMC) – a travel agency for the business travel market consisting of a call center and online sales

5. Online travel agency - an agency with a predominantly online presence and minimal call center activity

6. Online TMC or ITMC (Internet TMC) – an online agency for the business travel market

7. PAX is used when referring to the traveler in the airline industry.

8. Airline tariff publishing company – http://www.atpco.net/

9. http://www.sita.aero

10. The general public usually talks about three classes: First, business and economy/coach. However these are rather cabin classes and within a cabin there can be many more classes depending on the fare rules (i.e., non-refundable fare, mileage accrual, 60 days advance purchase, etc.) which are generally named with letter (i.e., C for business, etc.). Each airline uses letters differently for their Class Of Service (COS)

11. Wikipedia definition for Meta search engine: A Meta search engine is a search tool that sends user requests to several other search engines and/or databases and aggregates the results into a single list or displays them according to their source (http://en.wikipedia.org/wiki/Metasearch_engine). In travel meta search engines (e.g., sidestep.com, kayak.com, etc.) search the offerings of multiple websites and provide the user with a transparent overview. If the user wants to book an offer, there is a link to the originating site and a referral fee is paid by the supplier. In the beginning they were considered as a great way of shopping as they offer more search capabilities than OTAs. Recently some of them were discussed controversial as they seem to be biased

12. Opaque travel sites offer unsold inventory at discounted prices. The best example of this is priceline.com, where a hotel room night can be purchased by auction. One offers an amount for a room in a hotel of a particular star rating in

a specific area. However, one does not know whether one will get the room and in which hotel. This protects the regular hotel rates but at the same time finds purchasers for excess inventory

13   such as "Masterpricer" from Amadeus or "Bargainfinder" from Sabre

14   such as ITA Software's QPX (www.itasoftware.com), SITA

15   such as RapidReprice from Worldspan

16   IATA or ARC (www.arccorp.com); ARC belongs to 9 airlines and had 144 million transactions in 2008

17   Interlining (also known as "interline ticketing") is a voluntary commercial agreement between individual airlines to handle passengers traveling on itineraries that require multiple airlines (http://en.wikipedia.org/wiki/Interlining)

18   PNR - A PNR (Passenger Name Record) is an electronic record of all data and procedures related to a flight booking (or a hotel or rental car booking); the information is stored in the respective CRS for a particular period even after the flight

19   Technically they use separate partitions on the CRS

20   GDS - A GDS aggregates and manages booking records, also known as Passenger Name Records (PNRs), which it has received from the individual suppliers. Thus a GDS is made up of the CRS network and forms the basis of offer referral

21   Car Rental Management System - a computer reservation system for automobile and limousine rental

22   Property Management System - the hotel's computer reservation system

23   Carnit, an instrument for simultaneous, dynamic, usually computerized control of prices and capacity. In the beginning it was used by airlines, hotels and car rental agencies; in the meantime other sectors such as theater, cinema, concerts and many others apply it. Source: http://en.wikipedia.org/wiki/Yield_management

24   Customer Relationship Management (CRM) - a broadly recognized, widely-implemented strategy for managing and nurturing a company's interactions with customers, clients and sales prospects. http://en.wikipedia.org/wiki/Customer_relationship_management

25   i.e., http://www.aa.com/il8n/agency/General/aa_direct_connect.jsp provided by Farelogix

26 Consolidators such as CarTrawler and Rent-A-Car focus on the car sector by providing and selling bundled information about contingents and prices of the various individual car rental companies in their marketplaces

27 For example, Pegasus, HRS, Hotel.com, Hotel.de, Booking.com, etc.

28 Tour operators bundle the offerings of various travel companies (such as airlines, car rental companies and hotels) and offer a package price which may be significantly less than the individual prices, because, for example, the tour operator purchases large blocks of hotel capacity at fixed rates with better terms than individual travelers

29 For example, Farelogix

30 LCCs are low cost airlines which omit costly services and can fly with a high degree of efficiency, thus being able to offer low cost flights. For example: Southwest, Ryanair, JetBlue, Air Berlin

31 screen scraping - Screen scraping is part of data scraping which is a technique in which a computer program extracts data from human-readable output coming from another program. Originally, screen scraping referred to the practice of reading text data from a computer terminal's screen. Modern screen scraping techniques in the case of GUI applications include querying the graphical controls by programmatically obtaining references to their underlying programming objects. Source: http://en.wikipedia.org/wiki/Data_scraping#Screen_scraping. It is beneficial to ask for permission if you screen scrape web pages as providers might want to prevent screen scraping (e.g. Southwest does only allow a selected group of companies to screen scrape their site)

32 ElsyArres: http://www.elsyarres.com/, Partners: http://www.partners-software.com/

33 EMEA = Europe, Middle East and Africa

34 APAC = Asia Pacific

35 Figures from PhoCusWright and calculation by the author

36 SAS: Scandinavian Airlines

37 TWA - Trans World Airlines, US-amerikanische Fluggesellschaft

38 In the meantime, airlines have reduced their shares of Amadeus, Galileo was sold to the American hotel chain Cendant and Worldspan was taken over by

Citigroup Venture Capital. Today Galileo and Worldspan are part of the Travelport group brand

39   Source: Companies' real net output ratio: The strategic logic of Integration, Section 7.4 I

40   Only travel agencies which pay for each booking receive full access to all BA fares. Sabre introduced this model with the new BA contract. With Galileo, travel agencies must now pay one GBP instead of the previous 50 pence according to the online service "Travel Mole". Thus BA is rather expensive for travel agencies. www.touristikreport.de/rd/archiv/11034.php

41   Source: American Express – Diminishing Transparency of an opportunity for more of it: The EU Intends to Amend Regulations in the Global Distribution Systems (GDS) Market
http://corp.americanexpress.com/gcs/travel/us/docs/GlobalWhitePaper_ENG.pdf

42   full content - a complete overview of the content of all air fares

43   At the end of 2007, the EU presented a reform proposal for changing the code of conduct [REGULATION (EC) No. 80/2009] which has been in force since January 14, 2009. In the context of the regulation, a distinction is made between an owner and parent carrier

44   Parent carriers - airlines which directly or indirectly, alone or in concert with other airlines or rail companies, own or effectively control system providers

45   Code of conduct for parent carriers, in accordance with Regulation (EC) No 80/2009 of the European Parliament and of the Council – Code of Conduct, Article 10: "A parent carrier shall not, subject to reciprocity as referred to in paragraph 2, discriminate against a competing CRS by refusing to provide the latter, on request and with equal timeliness, with the same data on schedules, fares and availability relating to its own transport products as those which it provides to its own CRS or to distribute its transport products through another CRS, or by refusing to accept or to confirm with equal timeliness a reservation made through a competing CRS for any of its transport products which are distributed through its own CRS. The parent carrier shall be obliged to accept and to confirm only those bookings which are in conformity with its fares and conditions."

46   preferred fares - Fares which are made available to a select group of users via a GDS – so-called "preferred private fares". The price level of preferred fares is below that generally accessible via a GDS

47   Lufthansa press release, May 2009: Lufthansa and Sabre sign a long-term full content agreement;

http://de.eu.sabretravelnetwork.com/images/uploads/releases/PM_Sabre_Lufthansa_Distribution_Deal_2.pdf

48   eTN – global travel industry news, "All's fare in unbundling airline fees", www.eturbonews.com/5436/alls-fare-unbundling-airline-fees

49   Imagine that a beverage manufacturer wants to offer passengers a new drink at a special promotional price of 50 cents. In the old, code-based system, only static recurring products for which agents have been trained can be sold

50   Source: Oxford Economics, 2009 www. oxfordeconomics.com. Study commissioned by Oxford Economics, the U.S. Travel Association and the Destination & Travel Foundation. Source: Business Travel: A Sound Investment, 2009 http://meetingsmeanbusiness.com/value-meetings. Source: Procurement Travel, The Source for Managed Travel Insight, www.promedia.travel/nl/proc/metrics-html.php?isid=Sep-09

51   Principles of problem formation and problem resolution Paul Watzlawick, John H. Weakland, Richard Fisch, 1974 principles of problem formation and problem resolution Paul Watzlawick, John H. Weakland, Richard Fisch, 1974

52   some ideas are presented on how one can react flexibly despite this difficult, volatile and unpredictable market environment

53   Moore's Law states that the complexity of integrated circuits doubles about every two years with minimal component costs. Complexity was understood by Gordon Moore, who formulated the principle in 1965, to be the number of circuit components on a computer chip. Originally Moore spoke of a doubling each year, but in 1975 he corrected his statement to every two years (see also Wirth's Law). http://en.wikipedia.org/wiki/Moore%27s_law

54   "Travel Innovation and Technology Trends, 2010 and Beyond (Preview)", March 2010

55   Source: Organizational Behavior, Oxford University Press, 4th Edition by Robin Fincham & Peter Rodes

56   Fincham, Robin and Rhodes, Peter. Organizational Behavior, Oxford University Press, 4th edition. "Group and intergroup behavior"

57   Organizational Behavior, Oxford University Press, Section 15, "Organizational culture", Tom Burns, culture is unifying; page 535

58   Ibid., p. 529

59   Ibid., p. 275 ff

60 Ibid., p. 289 f

61 Total number of Internet users in the United States in 2008: 247,100,000. Total number of mobile Internet users in the United States: 78,800,000 (duration: 45 hours/week total - 38 hours/week stationary - 7 hours/week mobile)

62 http://148apps.biz/app-store-metrics/

63 GPS (Global Positioning System) is now firmly integrated in most mobile phones

64 Ticket exchange

65 Radio Frequency Identification already initiated by Apple for a travel application   http://www.patentlyapple.com/patently-apple/2010/04/itravel-apples-future-travel-centric-app-for-the-iphone.hmtl

66 Meeting duration: 1h; travel time there 3h, return travel 2.5 h, adds up to 7.5 hours. With virtual meetings: Set-up/dis mantling ½ h + 1 h meeting = five meetings in 7.5 hours

67 Before: one meeting per unit of time with a closing rate of 5 %. Now: five meetings per unit of time with a closing rate of 2.5 % results in a closing rate of 12.5 % for the same time period

68 e.g., Webex, meeting, go-to, etc.

69 1 tree = 6 kg/day = 2190 kg/year = 65,700 kg/30 years = 17 flights between Germany and Chile/30 years or the US to Australia; round-trip flight Germany Chile or LAX-SYD: 15,000 miles = 24,135 km = 3,861 kg CO_2

70 http://www.thomascook.com/sustainable-tourism/the-travel-foundation/#donations

71 corporate social responsibility (CSR) - a concept that serves as a basis for a company to integrate social and environmental issues in their corporate activities and in the interaction with stakeholders on a voluntary basis. Definition of the European Commission, Green Paper, http://europa.eu/documentation/official-docs/green-papers/index_de.htm
http://de.wikipedia.org/wiki/Corporate_Social_Responsibility

72 www.reisenews-online.de/2009/09/08/umweltschutz-und-soziale-verantwortung-bei-rezidor/

73 http://www.reducemyfootprint.travel/about/news/index.cfm;jsessionid=3e3014a806d71c50d4525e7f50f5e7913669?content_id=4AF83A8D-A9A3-6ED2-

FA17F38D418C3706&CFID=46010517&CFTOKEN=f8830d4cc4fa3891-EC08A474-A325-557D-861746BD8982587B&jsessionid=3e3014a806d71c50d4525e7f50f5e7913669

74 Non-profit organization Atmosfair, created from a joint research project of the German Federal Ministry for the Environment and Germanwatch http://www.atmosfair.de/index.php?id=62&L=33%252Findex.php%253Fid%253D156%2520class%253Dl

75 GfK: Association for Consumer, Market and Sales Research (Gesellschaft für Konsum-, Markt- und Absatzforschung)

76 According to a report by IdeaWorks cited in The Beat Newsletter, September 21, 2009

77 According to The Beat newsletter 6/29/2010, among U.S. carriers, Delta Air Lines by far takes in the most revenue for miscellaneous fees and charges, with USD 592 million in the March quarter, according to the Bureau of Transportation Statistics. American followed at USD 261 million, with US Airways at USD 238 million, Southwest at USD 168 million, United at USD 156 million and Continental at USD 143 million.
The data include "baggage fees, reservation change fees and miscellaneous operating revenue, including pet transportation, sale of frequent flyer award miles to airline business partners and standby passenger fees," but do not include "revenue from seating assignments and on-board sales of food, drink, pillows, blankets, entertainment, or any other ancillary items"

78 According to airline financial analyst Robert Herbst, cited in The Beat Newsletter, October 20, 2009

79 3M privacy filters survey of 806 adults over 18 – margin of error +/- 4%

80 There will be two types of EMDs: 1. EMDS - Standalone: (e.g. ground transportation, deposits); 2. EMDA - Associated EMDA: at the coupon level (dependent on E-ticket, e.g. lounge access; multiple EMDAs can exist for one ticket)

81 http://www.facebook.com/press/info.php?statistics

82 http://en.wikipedia.org/wiki/List_of_countries_and_dependencies_by_population_density

83 http://socialnomics.net/2009/08/11/statistics-show-social-media-is-bigger-than-you-think/

84 http://www.personalizemedia.com/garys-social-media-count/

85 User-Generated Content (UGC) for travel such as wikitravel, wikifacebook, tripadvisor, etc.

86 Intelligent agents - In artificial intelligence, an intelligent agent (IA) is an autonomous entity which observes and acts upon an environment (i.e. it is an agent) and directs its activity towards achieving goals (http://en.wikipedia.org/wiki/Intelligent_agent) . In the travel industry it can be computers which act like a human being and repeat searches and workflows efficiently and error free

87 SAP is a company headquartered in Germany (www.sap.com). "SAP" stands for Systems, Applications, and Products in Data Processing

88 Years to reach 50 million users: radio (38 years), TV (13 years), Internet (4 years), iPod (3 years). Facebook added 100 million users in less than 9 months. iPhone applications hit 1 billion in 9 months

89 http://www.patentlyapple.com/patently-apple/2010/04/itravel-apples-future-travel-centric-app-for-the-iphone.html

90 The active composition of an offer from multiple parts such as a flight, hotel reservation and car rental in a single-price package

91 Purchasing of a service – in this case vacancies

92 INFX format - a text file based on the standardized INFX interface in which the trips are made available according to date, room type, board and occupancy with sale prices. Each record is checked beforehand for allotment availability so that only dates which can be booked are read

93 Forrester Research 2008 and 2008

94 PhoCusWright report 2010: Phocuswright's analysis suggests that OTAs would have to increase ticket volume by 45-90 % to fully offset lost fees, and air bookings' share of OTA sales would have to increase from 32 % in 2008 to 46-61 % (versus 44 % OTA share at the peak in 2002)

95 assuming regulatory approval http://www.businessweek.com/news/2010-04-21/google-said-to-be-in-talks-to-buy-travel-company-ita-update1-.html

96 Thirty-three percent are booked offline via the TMC CWT and 17 % via Cliqbook, the corporate booking tool provided by the TMC

97 Payment card industry

98 http://news.cnet.com/8301-13579_3-10311907-37.html

99 http://www.thebeat.travel/blog/node/360

100 http://en.wikipedia.org/wiki/Napster

101 as of mid 2010: http://www.bloomberg.com/apps/quote?ticker=NOK1V%3AFH

102 as of mid 2010: http://www.bloomberg.com/apps/quote?ticker=AAPL%3AUS

103 http://www.bing.com/travel/

104 http://www.reuters.com/article/idUSTRE66050K20100702

105 First impressions of such a claim can be seen here: http://www.thebeat.travel/blog/downloads/leeches.pdf discussed controversially here: http://www.thebeat.travel/news.php?adate=jun_10&cid=IATA-GDS

106 http://www.huawei.com/publications/view.do?id=762&cid=662&pid=61

107 http://www.time.com/time/business/article/0,8599,1892845,00.html#ixzz0rTQr4Aba

Printed in Great Britain by
Amazon.co.uk, Ltd.,
Marston Gate.